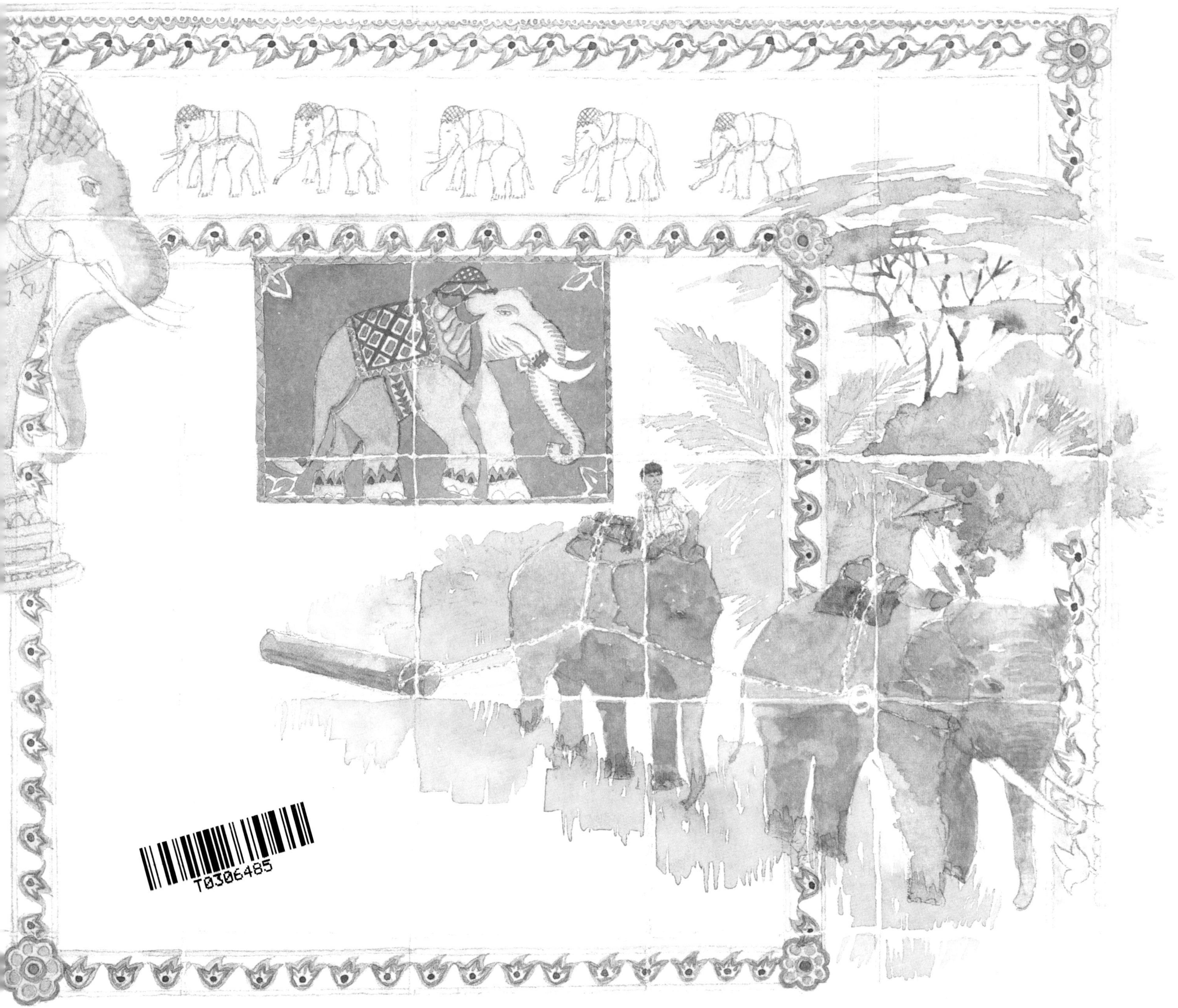

The Thai Silk Sketchbook

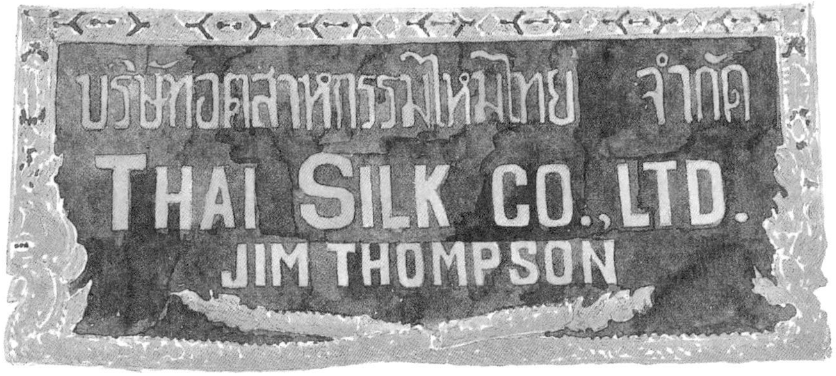

Published to commemorate the 30th anniversary
of the opening of the Jim Thompson
Thai silk shop at 9 Surawong Road, Bangkok

Acknowledgments

This book developed as a project after I had done a series of paintings of Jim Thompson's famous house on the klong in Bangkok. Once these were completed, the idea of a book on the life and legend of Jim Thompson and his company was a natural succession.

I would like to acknowledge thanks to my friend Bill Booth, Managing Director of Jim Thompson Thai Silk Company, who encouraged me with this sketchbook from the beginning; to Gerald Pierce, Jim Thompson's Design Director, for his invaluable help; and to William Warren for writing with such in-depth knowledge of the subject.

Thanks go also to the innumerable staff of the company who helped me in the research of silk making, with the wonderful politeness of Thai hospitality one has come to respect.

Finally to my publisher, Didier Millet, and my editor Tim Jaycock, who so patiently have helped me in the making of this book.

First published 1997
Reprinted 2006, 2017, 2019

Published by Editions Didier Millet
52 Genting Lane #06-05
Ruby Land Complex 1, Singapore 349560
www.edmbooks.com.sg

Creative Director: Graham Byfield
Editor: Tim Jaycock
Art Director: Tan Tat Ghee
Designer: Lee Woon Hong
Production Manager: Annie Teo

Color separation in Singapore by Pica Digital
Printed in Malaysia by SSP Industries Sdn. Bhd.

ISBN: 978-981-3018-93-8

ELEMENTARY CHLORINE FREE · LONG-LIFE ISO 9706 · RECYCLABLE

Printed on 160gsm Modigliani Neve

JIM THOMPSON

The Thai Silk Sketchbook

Watercolors by Graham Byfield

Text by William Warren

EDITIONS DIDIER MILLET

Jim Thompson - The Legend

Page 6: Bangkok, Glittering City of Angels

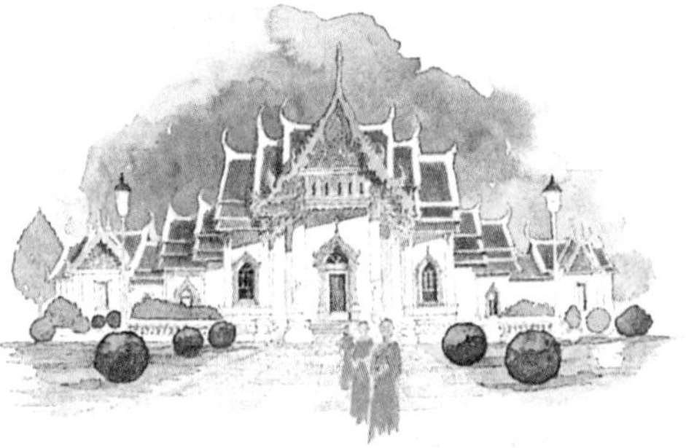

Page 13: Fascinating Markets, Smiling People

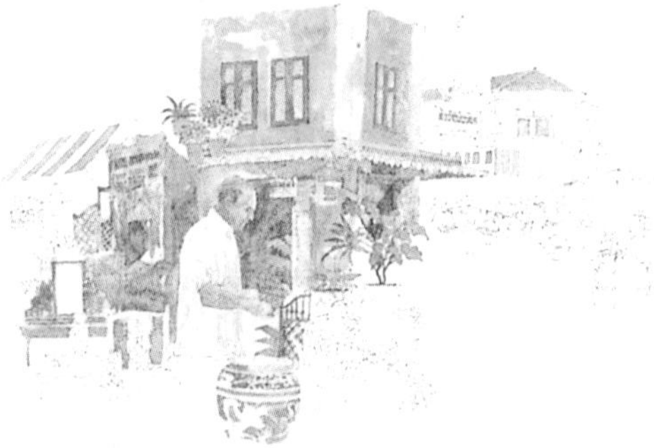

Page 24: The House on the Klong

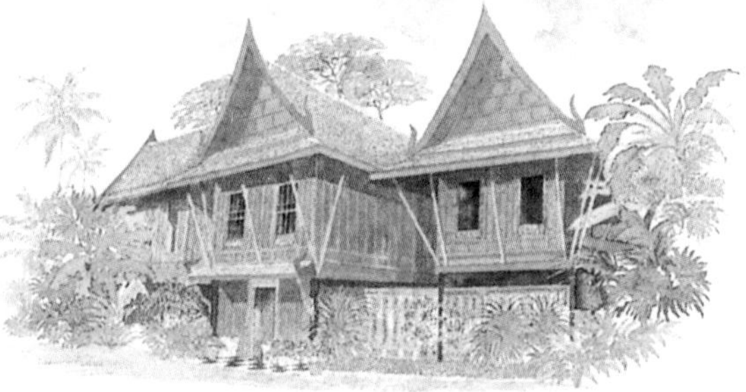

Page 38: Moonlight Cottage

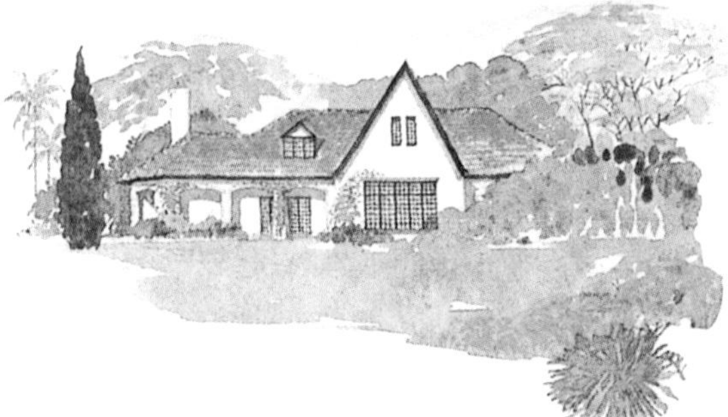

The Making of Thai Silk

Page 40: Where it all Started

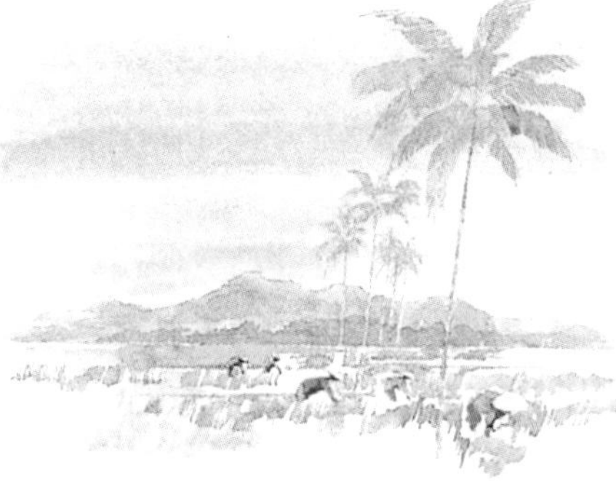

Page 44: The Traditional Way of Making Silk

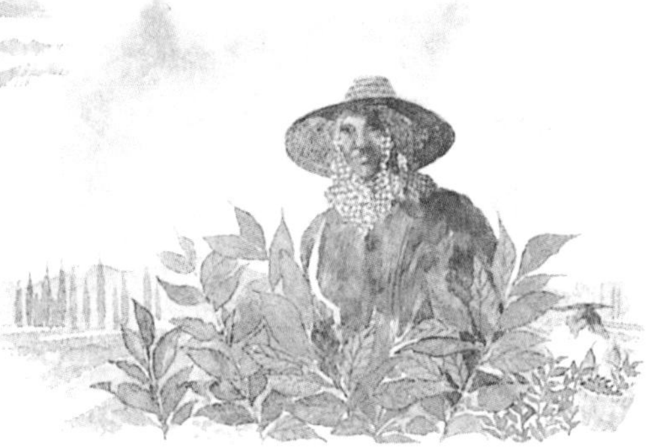

Page 66: The Traditional Use of Thai Silk

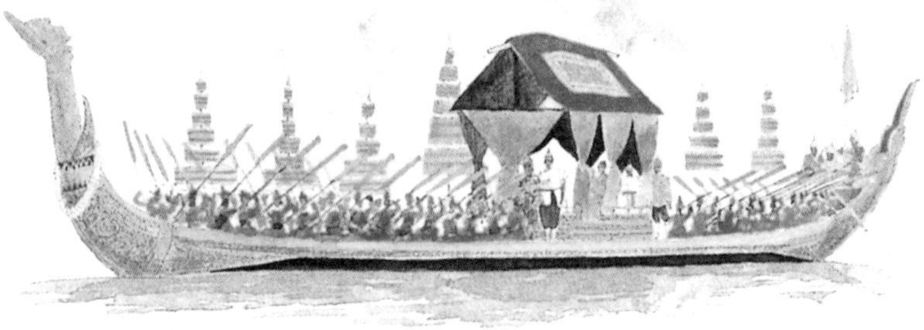

Page 68: The Bangkok Flagship

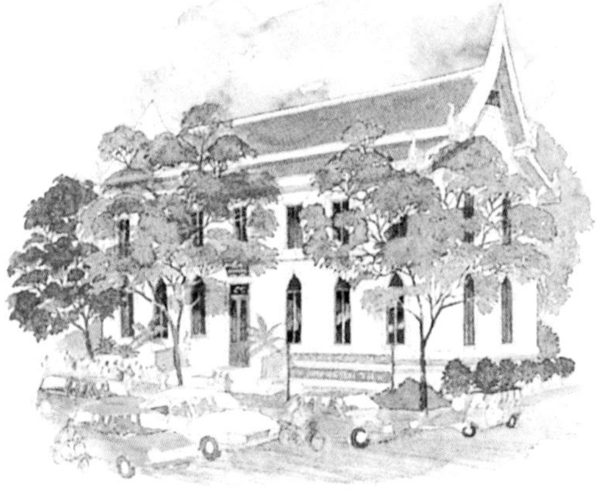

JIM THOMPSON — THE LEGEND

Bangkok, Glittering City of Angels

Even today, for all its towering modern buildings and notoriously congested streets, Thailand's capital still offers a surprising number of exotic sights: fabulous Buddhist temples and royal palaces that glitter like jewels in the tropical sunlight; shady *klongs*, or canals, that meander largely unnoticed through the city's heart; teeming markets piled high with temptations. Half a century ago, when our story begins, these impressions tended to predominate and they captivated more than a few romantic travelers who found themselves in what was then a remote and little-known kingdom.

The focus of Bangkok life in those days, as it had been since the city's founding in 1782, was the broad Chao Phraya River. On Rattanakosin Island, created by digging a canal at a point where the river made a sharp curve, King Rama I had built his Grand Palace, a fantasy world of gilded spires and classic Thai buildings that also contained the sacred Temple of the Emerald Buddha, guardian of the kingdom's fortunes. A community of Chinese traders was established downriver, outside the city walls, where they formed the nucleus of what became Bangkok's Chinatown. In 1945, this network of narrow, clamorous streets and alleyways was still the center of trade as well as the place to go in search of such treasures as a piece of Ming porcelain, a workable water pump, or an electric ceiling fan.

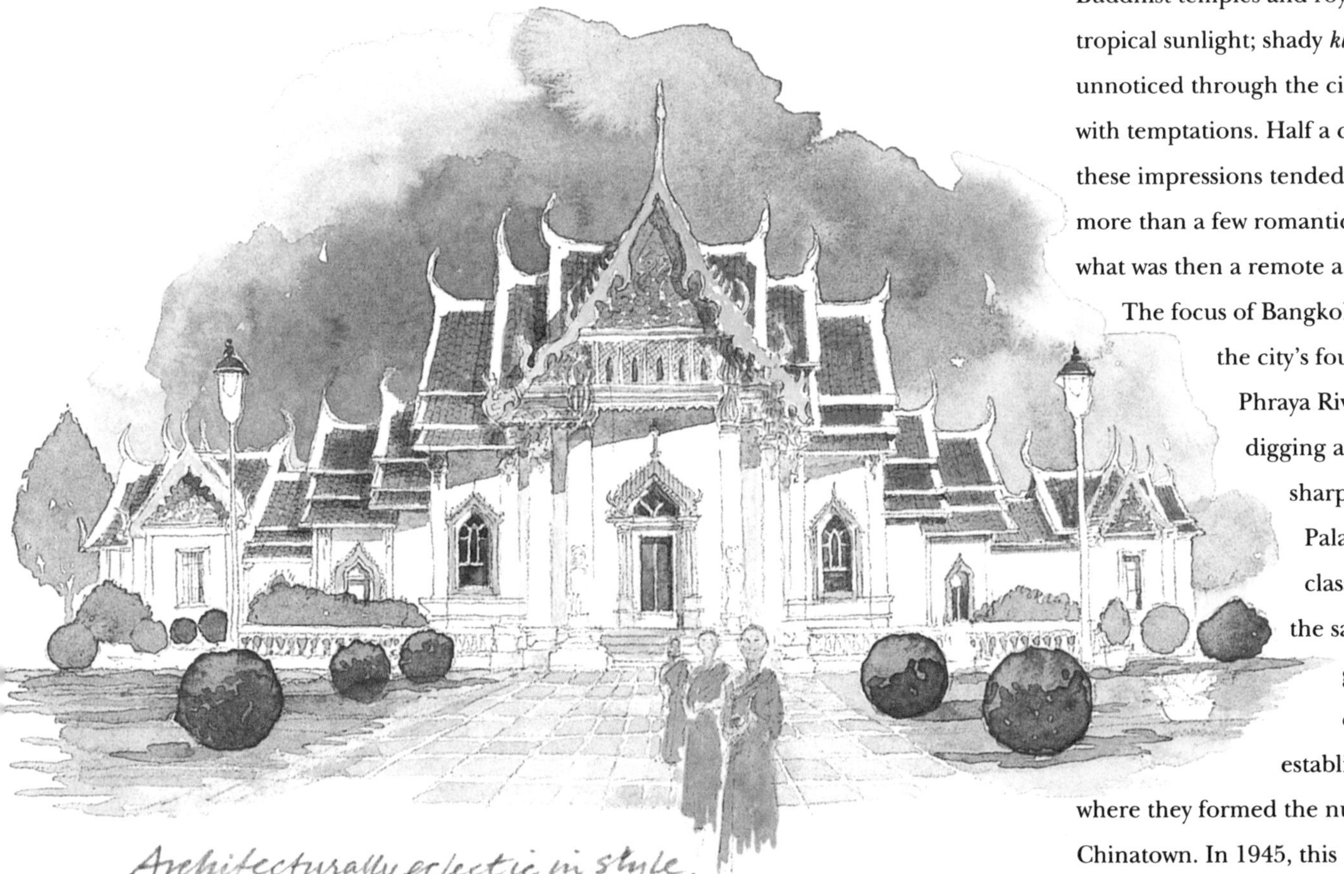

Architecturally eclectic in style, Wat Benchamabopit, the Marble Temple, was built in the early years of the 20th Century.

The Prasat Phra Thep Bidorn, part of the Temple of the Emerald Buddha complex in the Grand Palace, contains statues of previous Chakri Kings. The Emerald Buddha itself is the most venerated Buddha image in the kingdom, a symbol of national unity and independence.

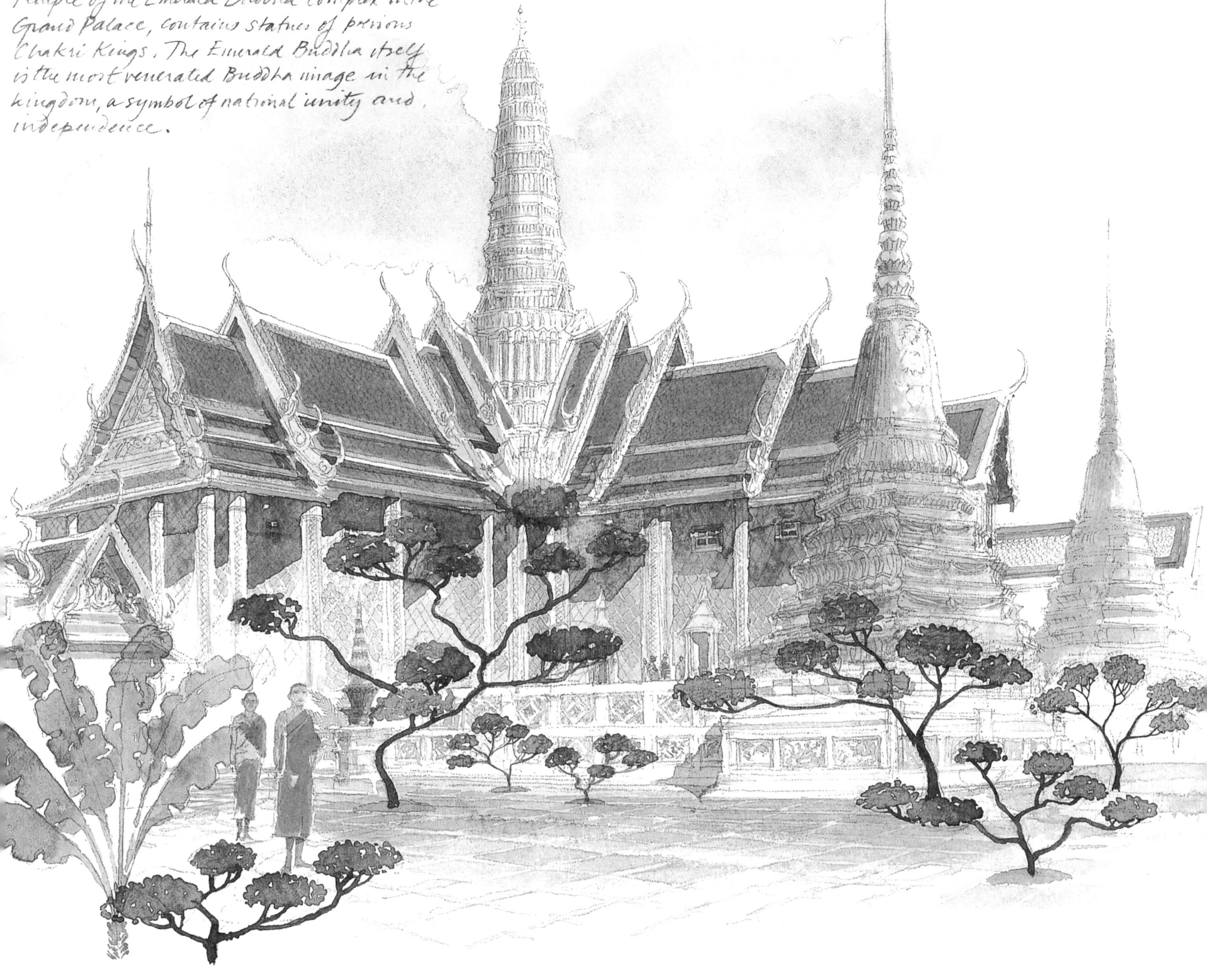

The central tower of Wat Arun, the Temple of Dawn, is 343 feet high and is adorned with fragments of multicolored porcelain. For a century and a half it has been a landmark on the Chao Phraya river and is passed by a daily stream of crafts that range from barges to swift, slender "hong yao" - long-tailed boats used as taxis.

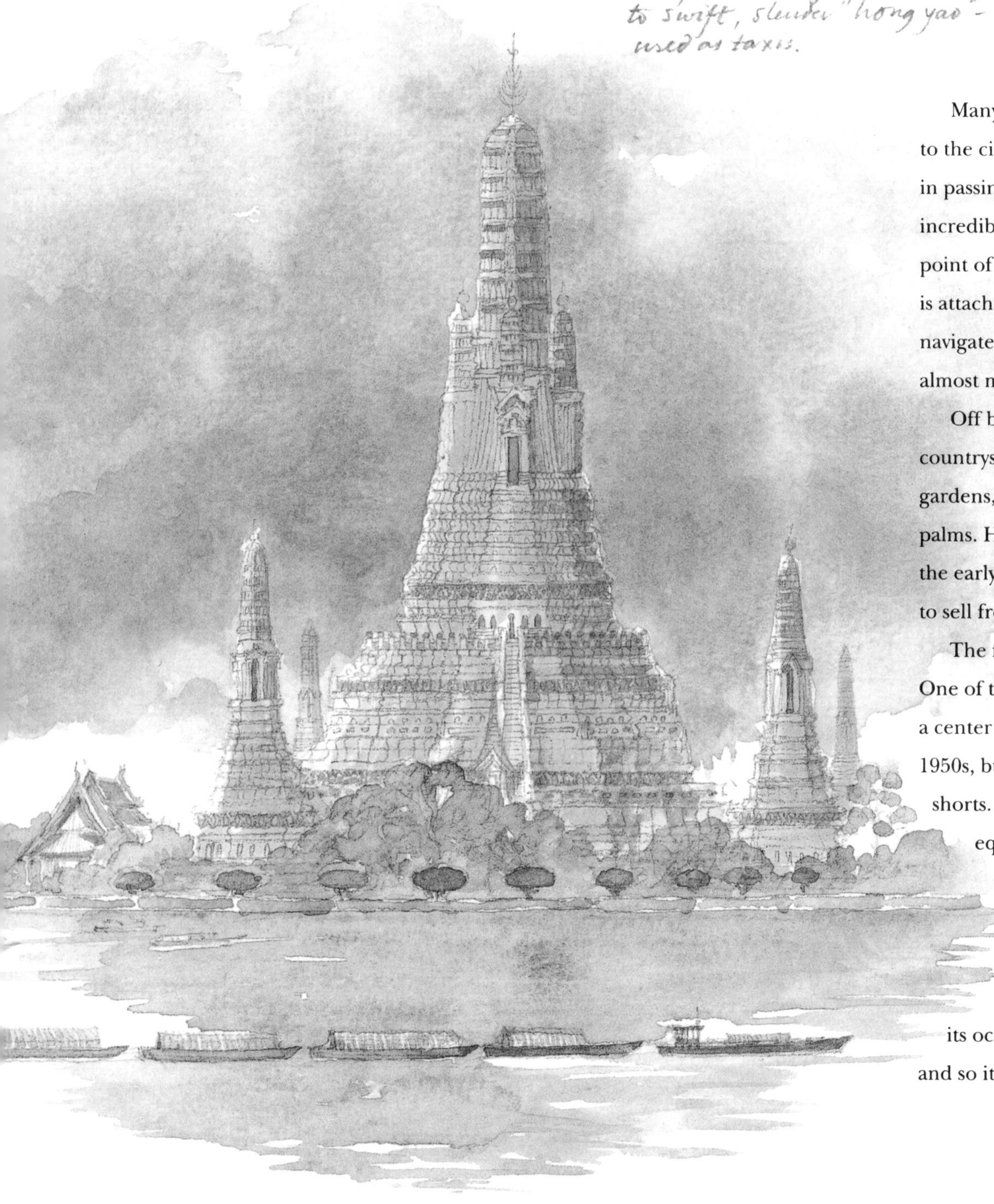

Many of the temples that added — and still add — so much to the city's atmosphere were also on or near the river. Glimpsed in passing from a mundane contemporary street, these incredible structures inspire a gasp of wonder; from the vantage point of a long-tail motor boat — so called because the propeller is attached to a long moveable pole that enables the boat to navigate in shallow canals and rice fields — they possess an almost magical power.

Off both banks of the river canals ran for miles into the countryside, past steep-roofed traditional Thai houses, market gardens, fruit orchards, plantations of coconut and betel-nut palms. Here, too, were the celebrated floating markets, where in the early morning hours hundreds of vendor boats congregated to sell fresh produce and prepared foods.

The first proper streets appeared in the mid 19th century. One of them, New Road, running parallel to the river, remained a center for European businessmen and tourists well into the 1950s, bustling with pedicabs manned by sturdy drivers in blue shorts. Banished in 1959, the pedicab was replaced by the equally jaunty *tuk tuk*, a three-wheeled motorized version just as adept at weaving through traffic.

An orderly, well-planned, predictable city, Bangkok never was. But it was full of color and vitality and serendipitous discovery, a place that for all its occasional frustrations was never for a moment boring; and so it remains in a new and very different time.

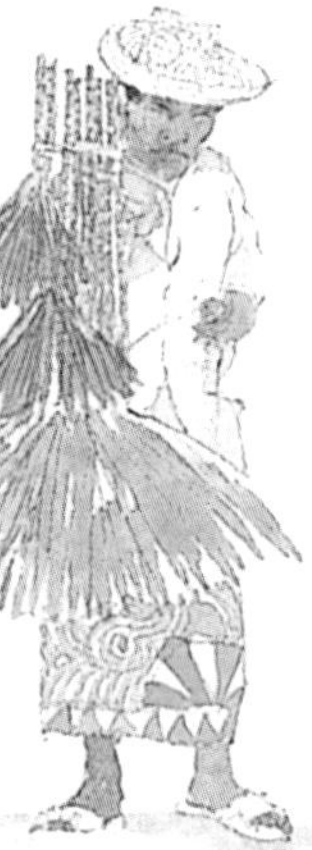

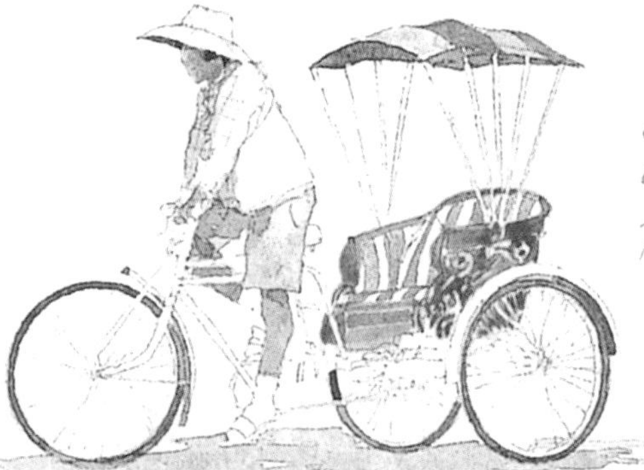

The pedicab may still be seen in a few outlying areas of Bangkok, while vendors of all kinds are a familiar part of street life.

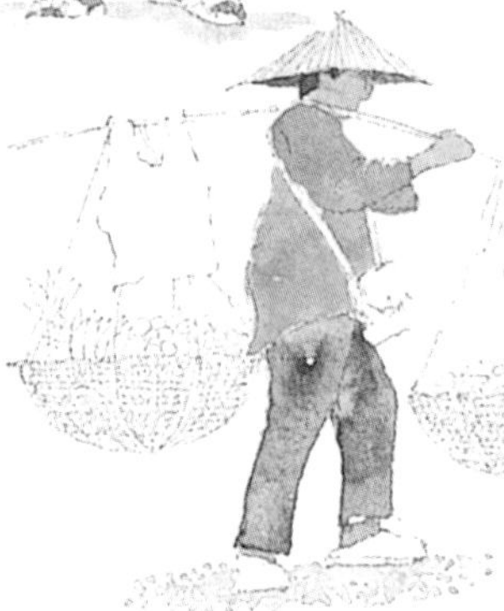

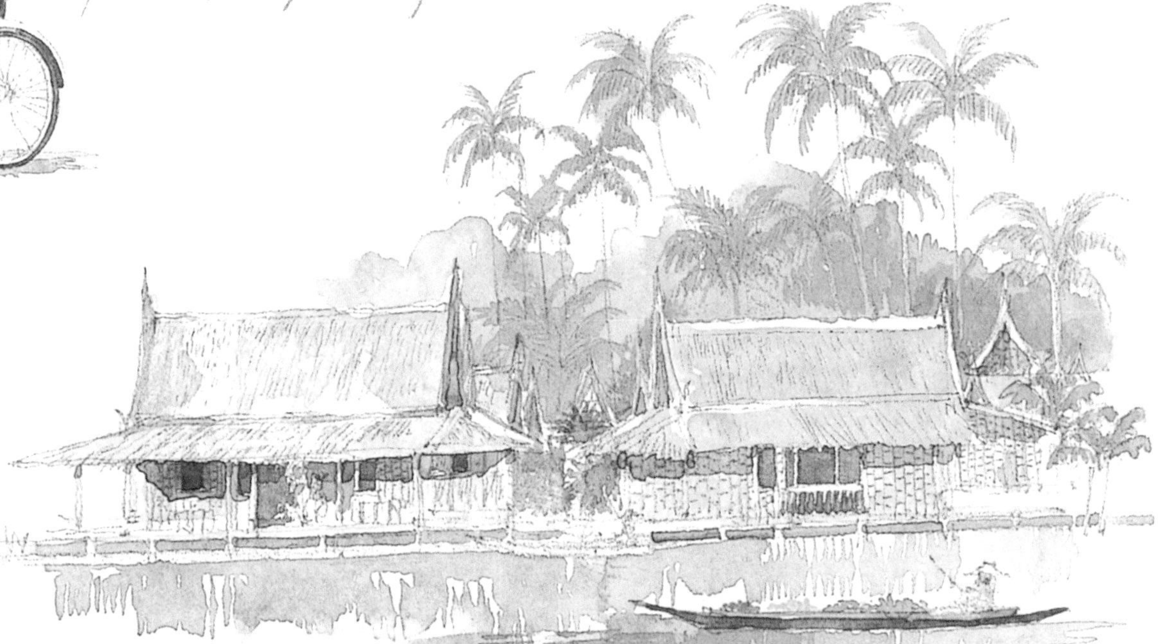

In addition to large and small public markets, oating markets – relics of Bangkok's ast – may still be found in longs and other water- ays, not far from the ty's modern center.

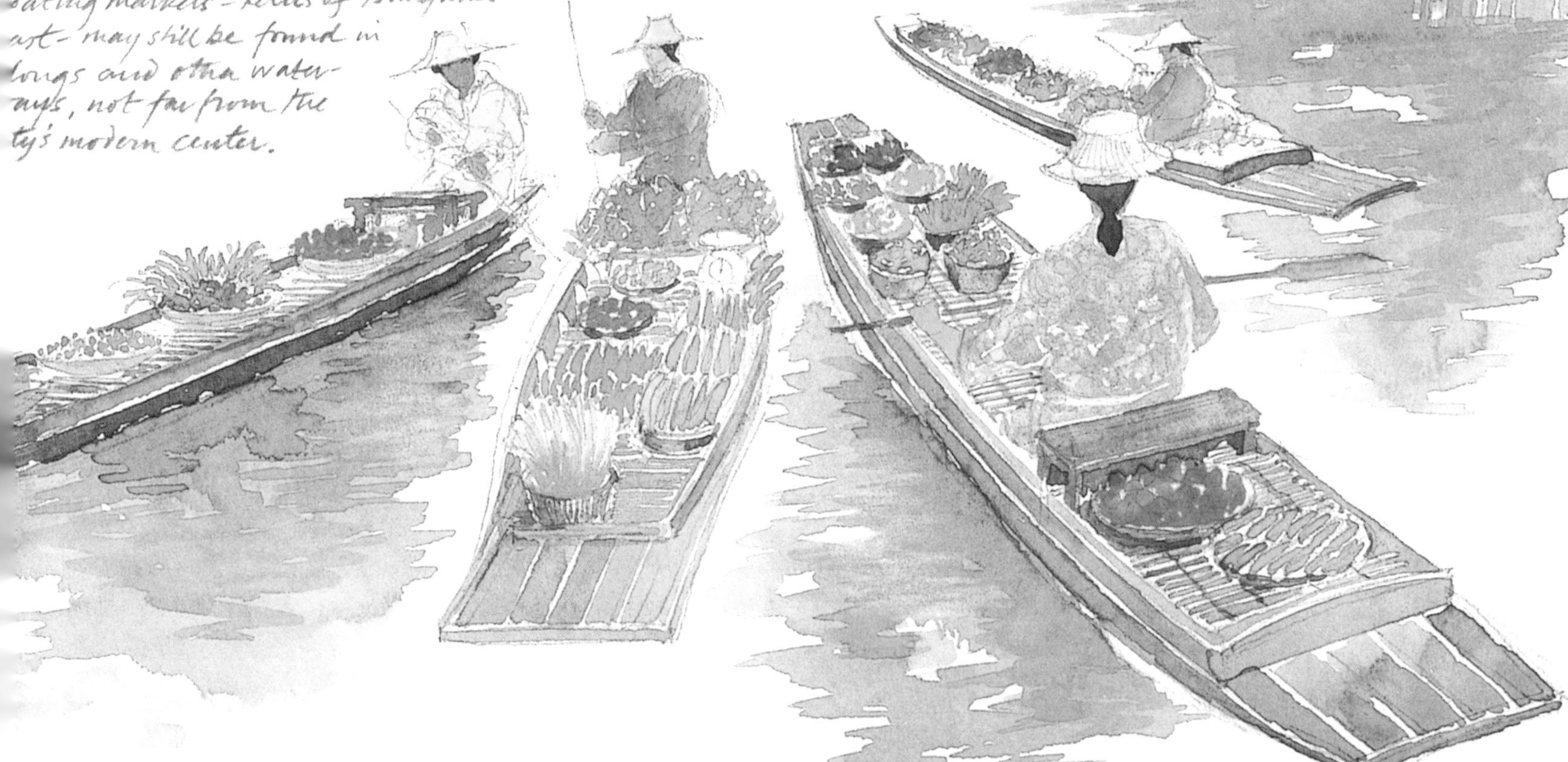

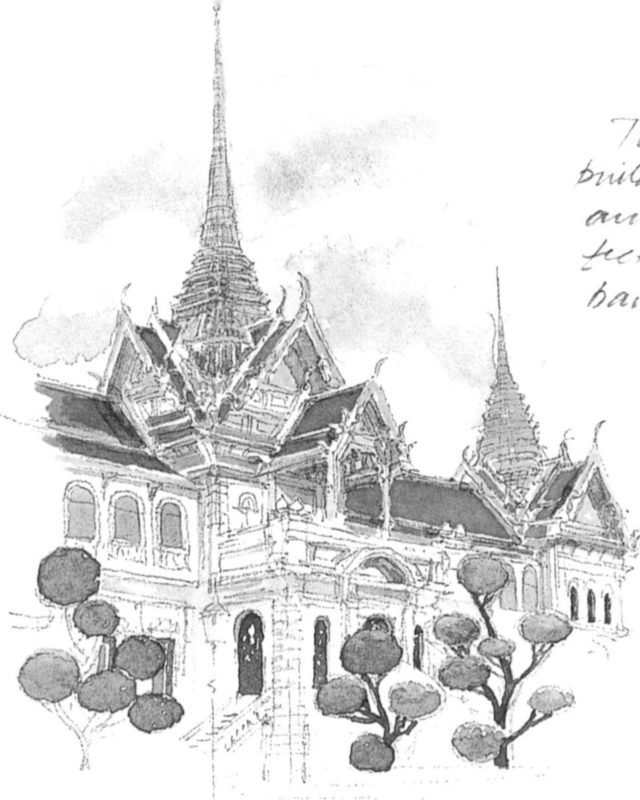

The Chaksi Maha Prasat, one of the largest buildings in the Grand Palace, dates from 1882 and is a blend of Thai and Western architectural styles. It is now used for Royal banquets and receptions.

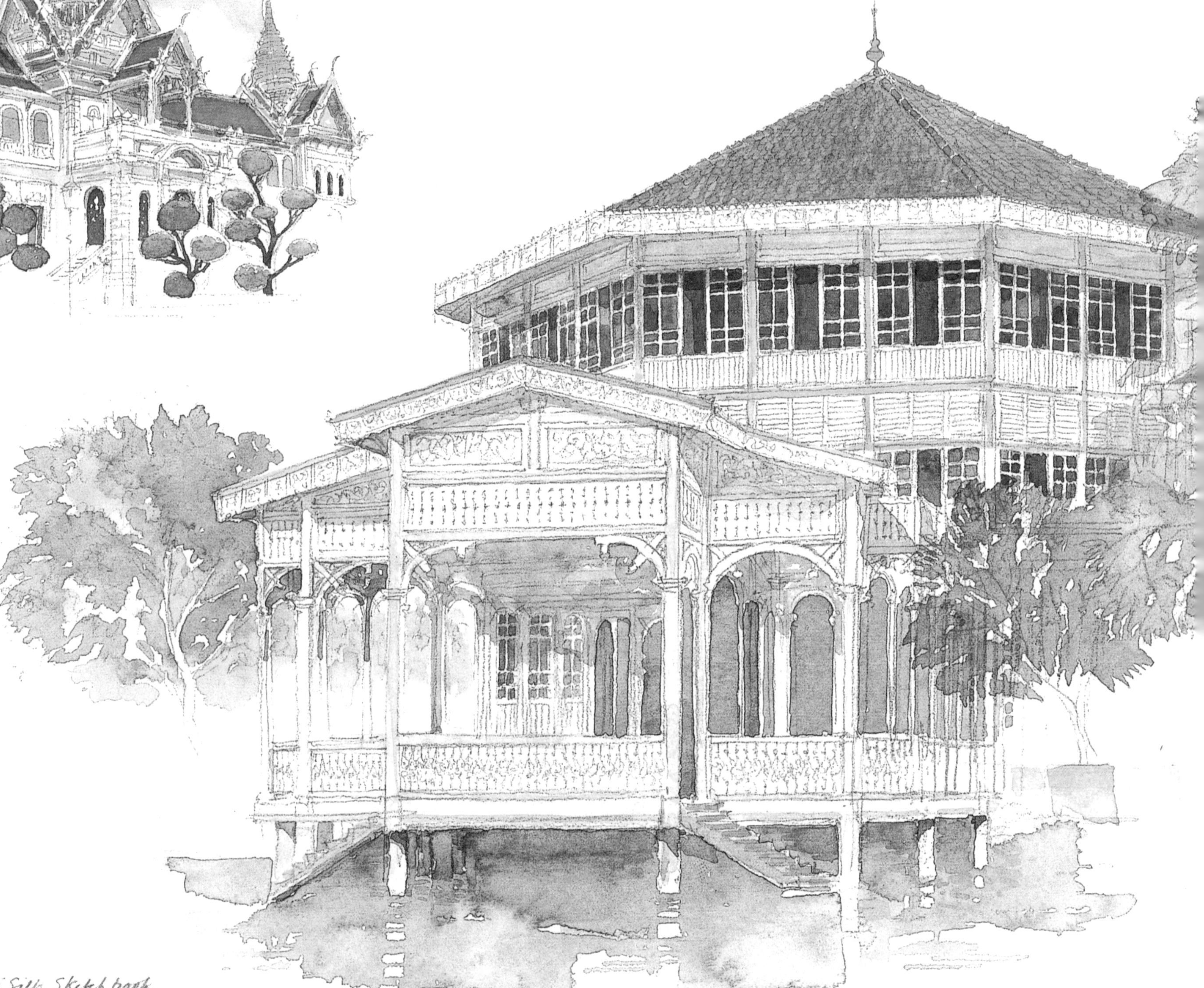

Vimarn Mek Palace, built in the reign of King Rama V, is an airy mansion constructed entirely of golden teak. Restored by the present Queen for Bangkok's Bicentennial in 1982, it is now a museum.

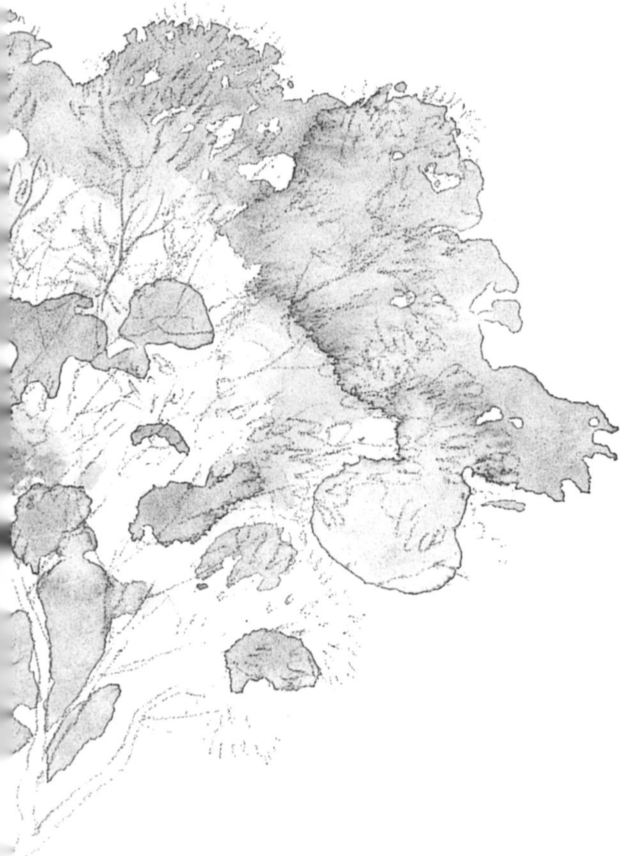

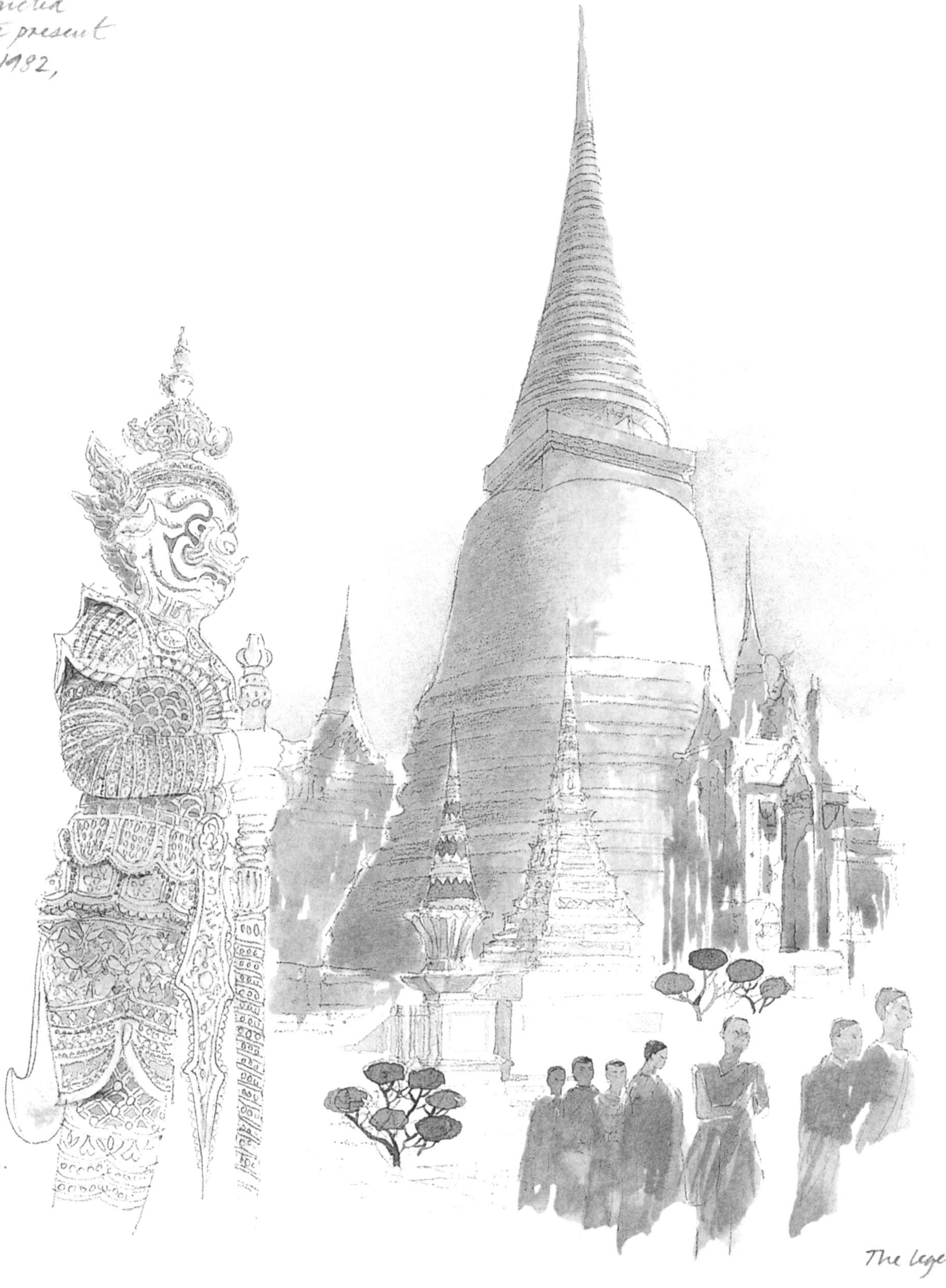

The Golden Stupa, part of the Temple of the Emerald Buddha in the Grand Palace compound, was modeled on a similar one in the ancient capital of Ayutthaya. It stands amid other buildings that are striking examples of Thailand's traditional artistic heritage.

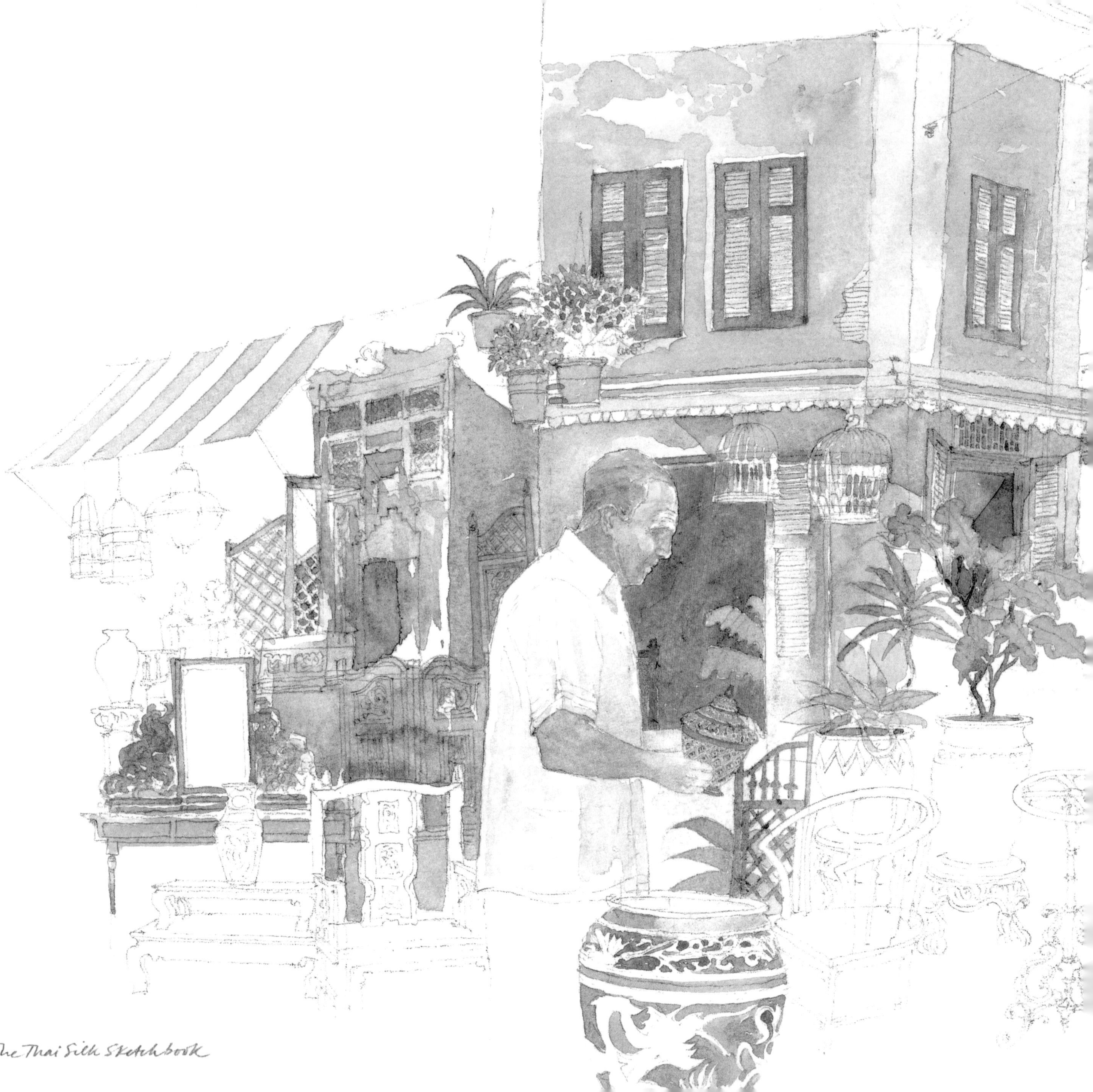

Jim Thompson began assembling his famous antique collection while browsing in Bangkok's older markets. Some of these areas are little changed today, as visitors in search of a bargain soon discover.

Fascinating Markets, Smiling People

In August of 1945, a few days after the end of World War II, the man whose name was to become almost synonymous with Thai silk stepped off a military plane at Bangkok's Don Muang Airport. He was an unlikely candidate for such a role. Nearing 40 years of age, James H.W. Thompson was a native of Delaware in the United States, an architect by profession with no previous experience of textile manufacture or design. He had spent most of the war working with the Office of Strategic Services (OSS) in North Africa and Europe; in 1945, he was transferred to Ceylon (now Sri Lanka), where preparations were underway to invade Thailand, which technically at least was at war with the Allies.

Japan's sudden surrender ended the need for invasion, and because the United States had refused to recognize Thailand's declaration of war in 1942, Thompson and his party — the first to arrive in Bangkok — came not as conquerors but as liberating friends. He found a world unlike any he had known before, one of smiling people and fascinating markets, of glittering temples and ancient ruins, of what he perceived as widely varied opportunities. When his military service came to an end, he was unwilling to leave it and decided instead to stay on and start some sort of business.

The traditional silk then being produced in small quantities, mostly for personal use, was not his first career choice, though he had already been attracted to pieces he came across and had sent some home to friends he felt would appreciate their

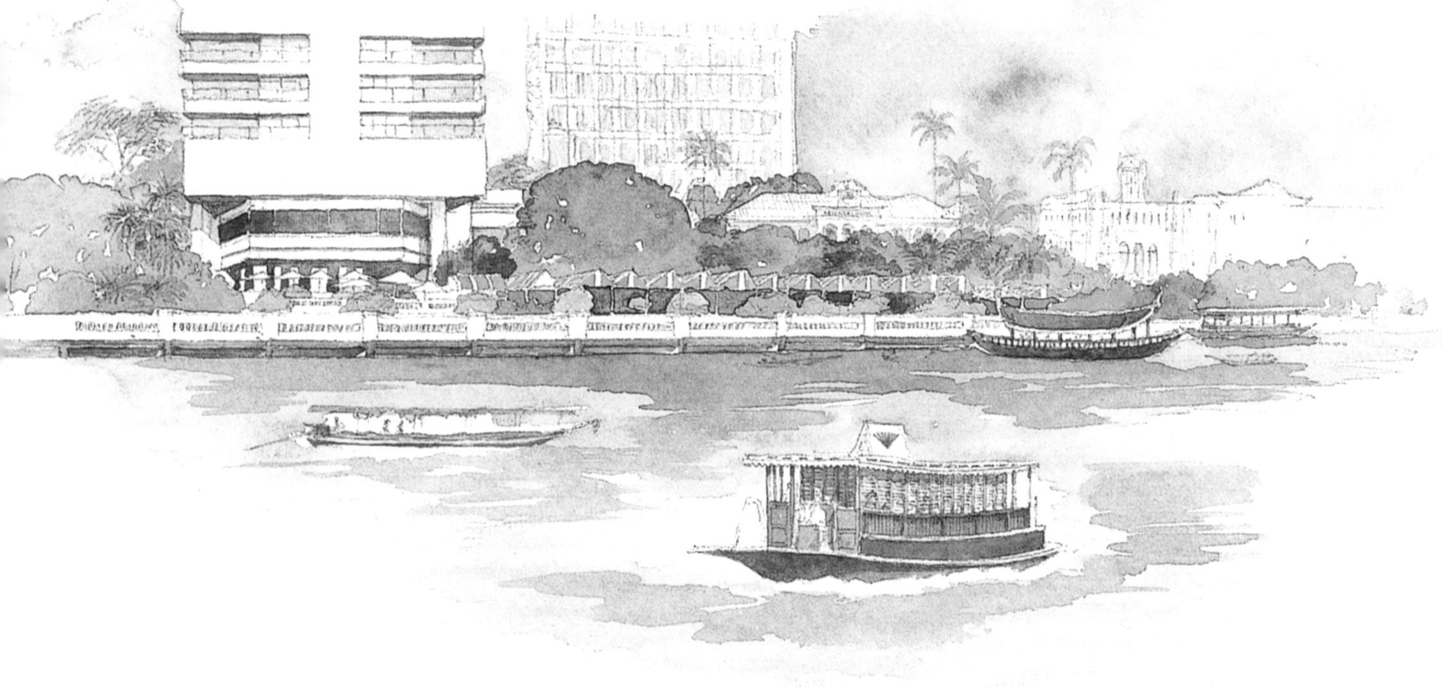

The Oriental Hotel today, as seen from the Chao Phraya river. An endless procession of varied river traffic can be viewed from the hotel terrace.

homespun texture and often surprising color combinations. Instead, he became a part of a venture to restore the venerable Oriental Hotel, which at the time was serving as billets for military personnel.

The Hotel by the River

For an architect with a taste for history, it was a logical choice. The Oriental was one of Asia's legendary hotels, an elegant structure overlooking the broad Chao Phraya River that had been built in 1887 on the site of an older facility. Before the war, nearly every visitor of importance had stayed there, from royalty to wandering writers like Somerset Maugham, and it was also a center for local society. It had suffered under the Japanese and in 1945 its amenities were sadly deficient, but with peace the visitors would be returning; there was no reason to doubt that it could once again become Bangkok's premier establishment.

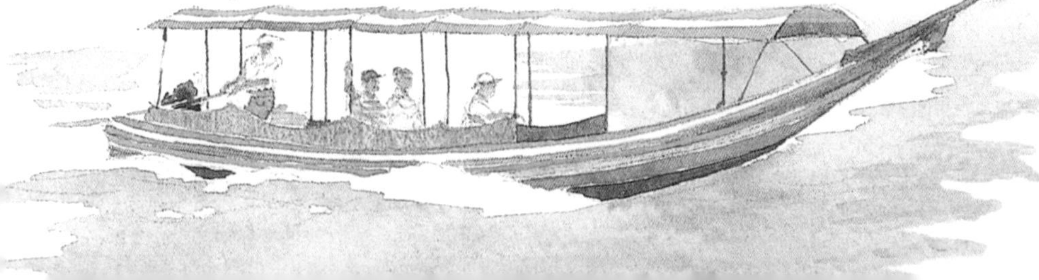

This would indeed happen — the Oriental today is regularly ranked among the world's top hotels — but without Thompson's participation. A disagreement with his partners led to his withdrawal and while he continued to live there for several years, he did not become involved again until the mid-1960s when he was asked to design the luxurious suites in the old Author's Wing.

Once he began to consider the commercial possibilities of Thai silk, he followed the idea up with determination. He collected all the pieces he could find in various out-of-the-way Bangkok shops and on trips upcountry, especially to the Northeast. He studied old silks in the National Museum and asked Thai and Laotian friends about techniques. The latter were especially helpful since many had relatives in the Northeast region who were actually weaving the fabric.

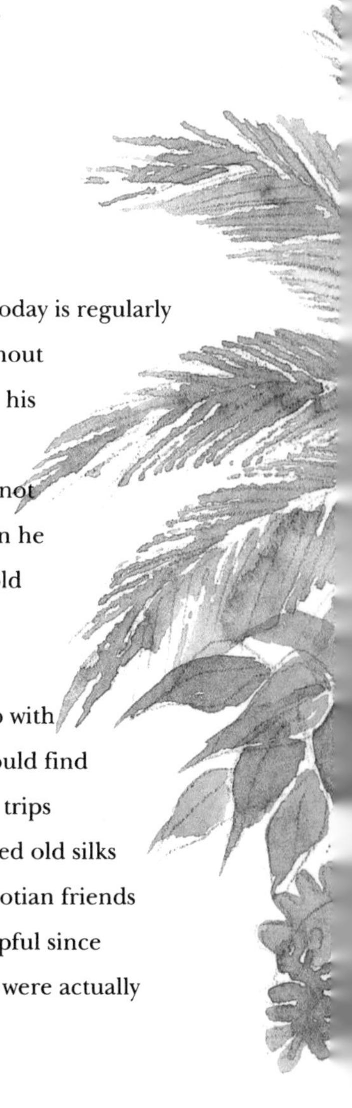

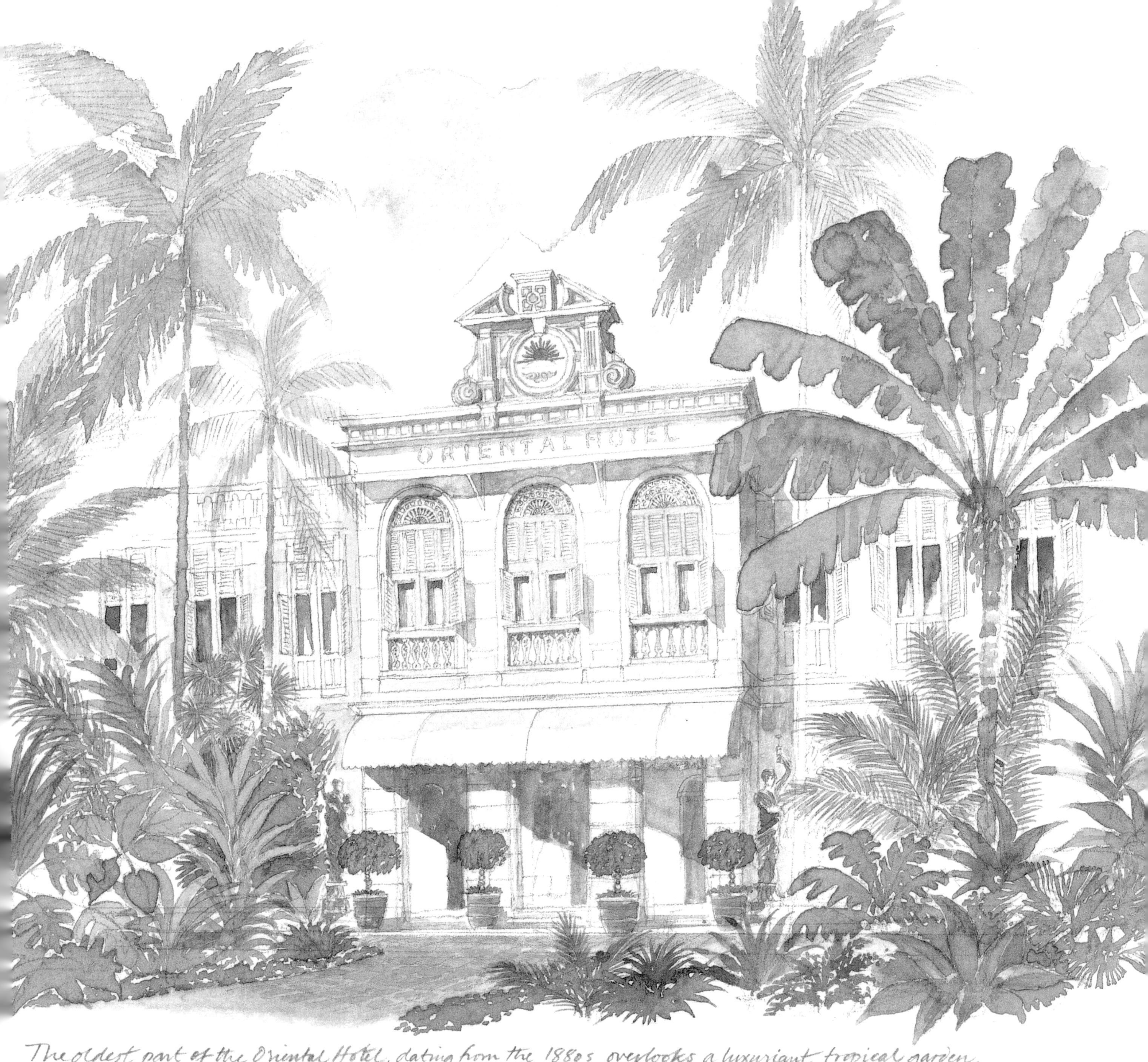

The oldest part of the Oriental Hotel, dating from the 1880s, overlooks a luxuriant tropical garden.

A significant step was taken when Thompson discovered an enclave of Thai Muslim weavers who lived in a place called Bangkrua in the heart of Bangkok. With its rickety boardwalks, mostly makeshift houses (though a few were in traditional Thai style), and wooden shops opening onto a murky *klong*, or canal, Bangkrua was perilously close to being a slum. But wonderful silks were still being created on its open verandahs, and many of its residents were gifted in skills that had been handed down for generations within the tightly knit community. One resident, a part-time plumber, was sufficiently intrigued by Thompson's enthusiasm to agree to weave a few unusually long pieces so that their potential could be tested with foreign buyers.

Other samples came from the northern city of Chiang Mai, where a few specialists made silk brocades by painstaking techniques that required weeks or even months to produce a single length for a woman's sarong. Some of these, too, were added to the growing collection with which he planned to make an impression on New York's sophisticated world of taste makers.

This notable event took place in early 1947, in the offices of *Vogue* magazine, and the results were encouraging. Not only was Edna Woolman Chase, the magazine's influential editor, enormously impressed by the dazzling colors of the unknown fabric (according to his often-repeated account, she dramatically summoned all the staff members to come and view the discovery); she also took more practical steps, showing it to various fashion designers and encouraging them to use it.

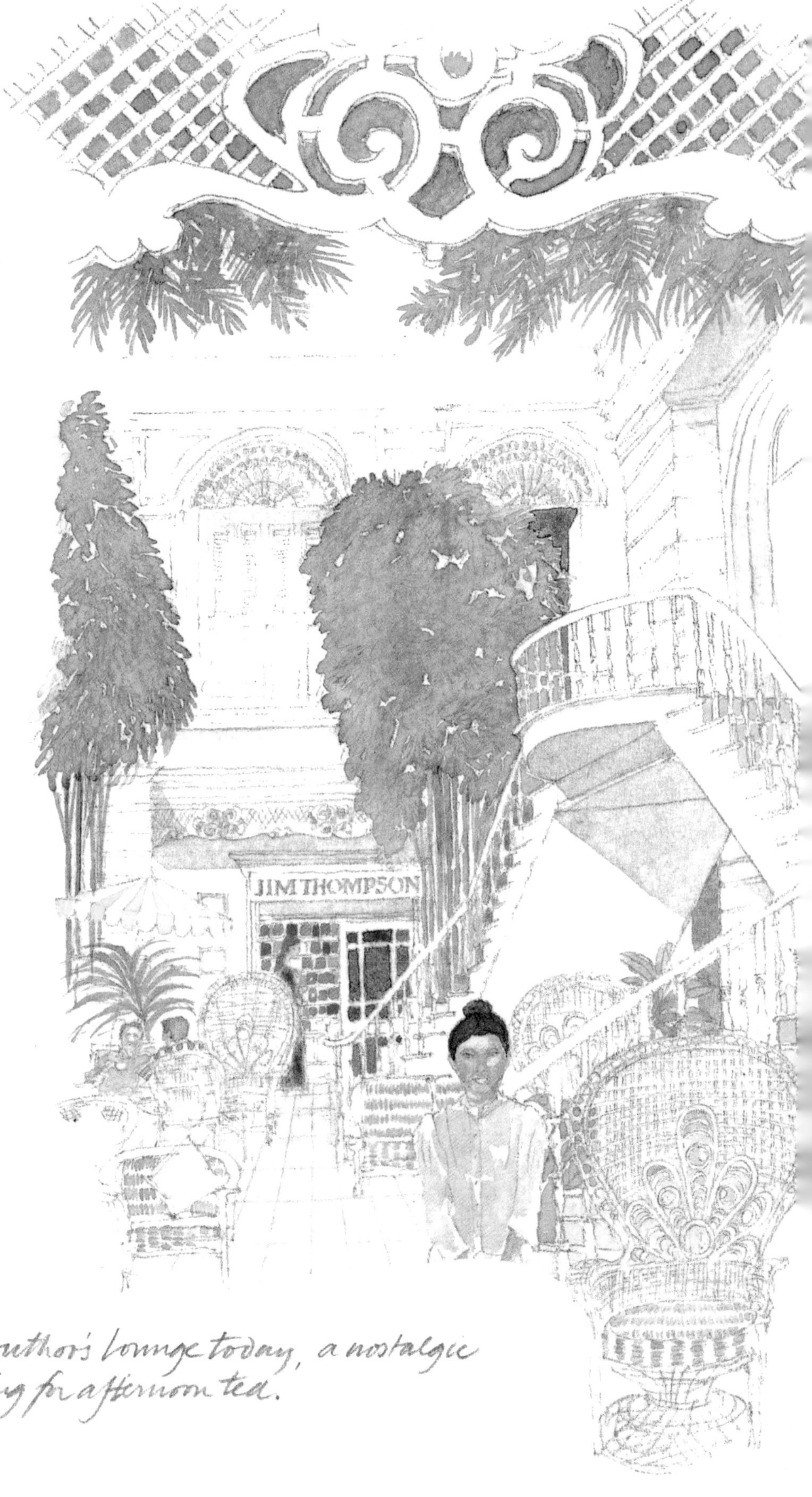

The Author's lounge today, a nostalgic setting for afternoon tea.

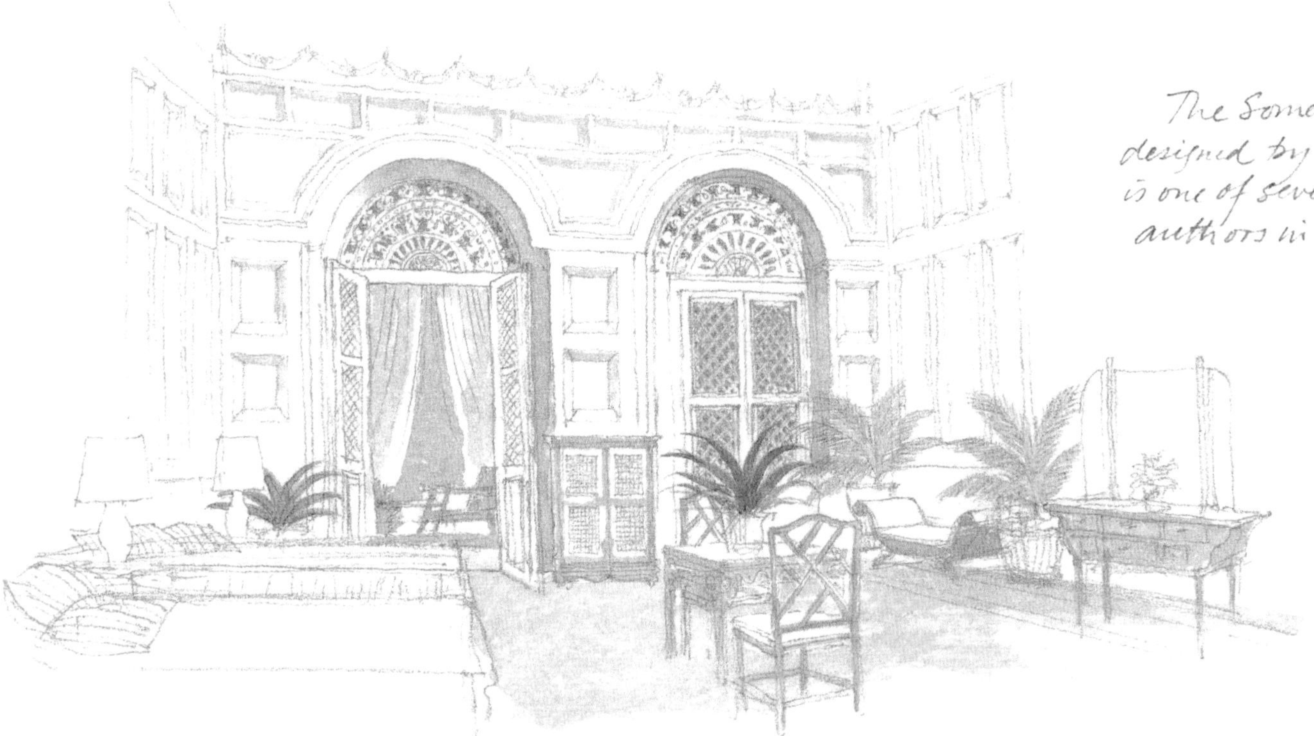

The Somerset Maugham Suite, designed by Jim Thompson in 1962, is one of several named after famous authors in the old wing of the hotel.

For Jim Thompson in the late 1940s, the Oriental lobby was a convenient place to display his dazzling silks.

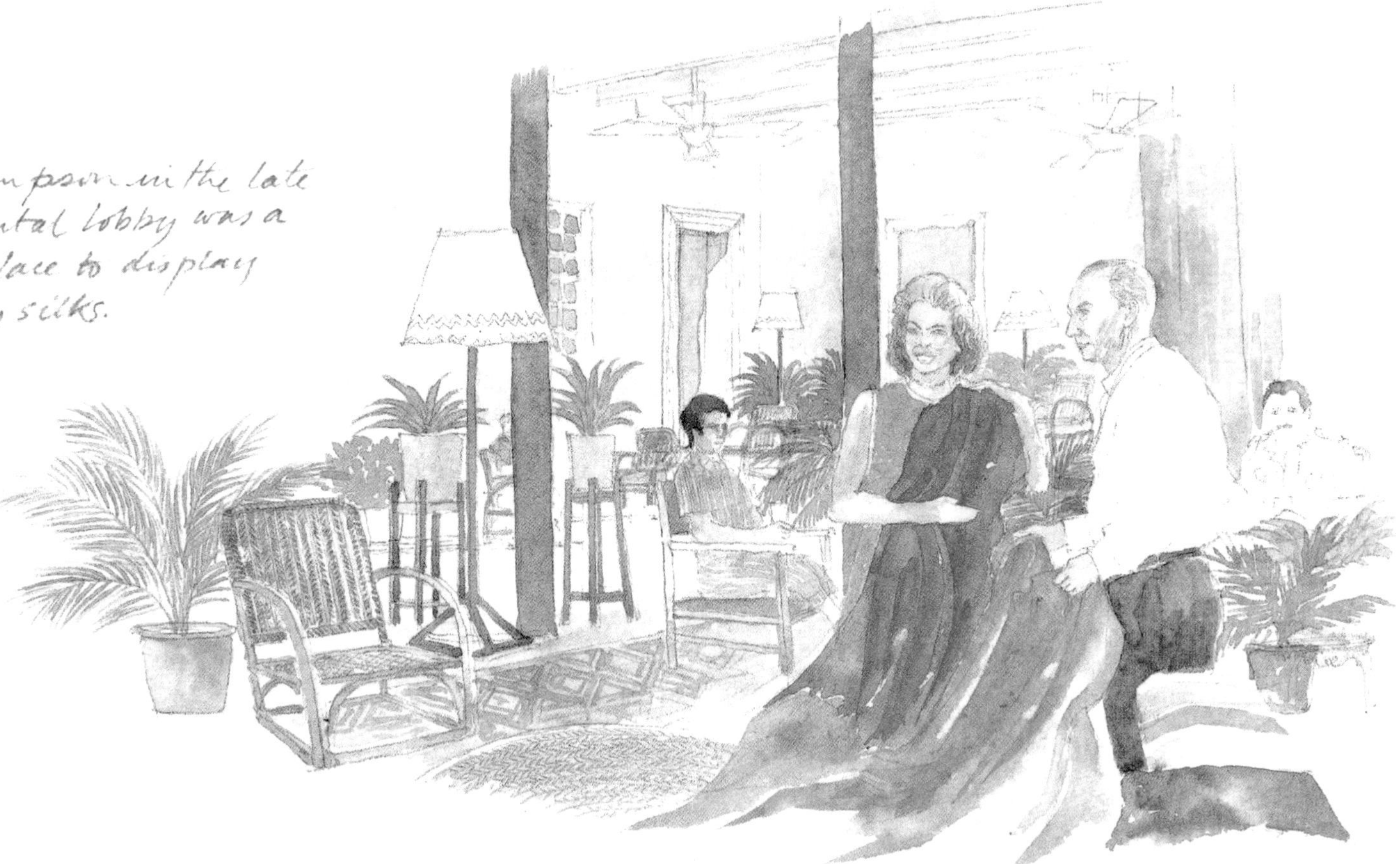

Some of the costumes produced by designer Irene Sharaff for "The King and I," a showcase for Jim Thompson silk that resulted in worldwide publicity and a flood of new orders.

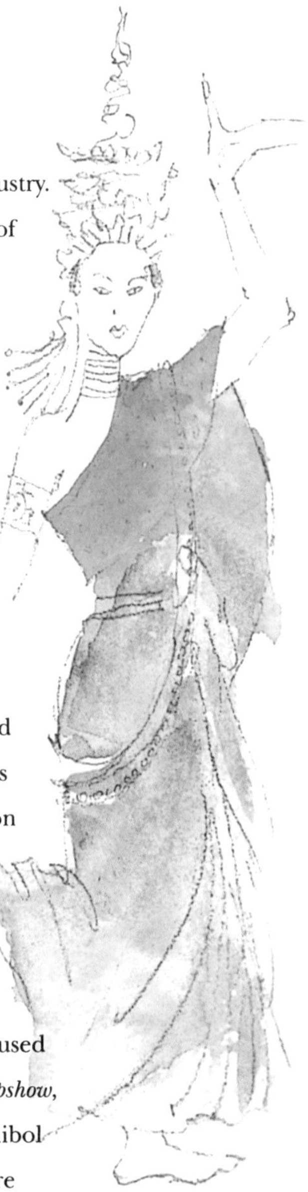

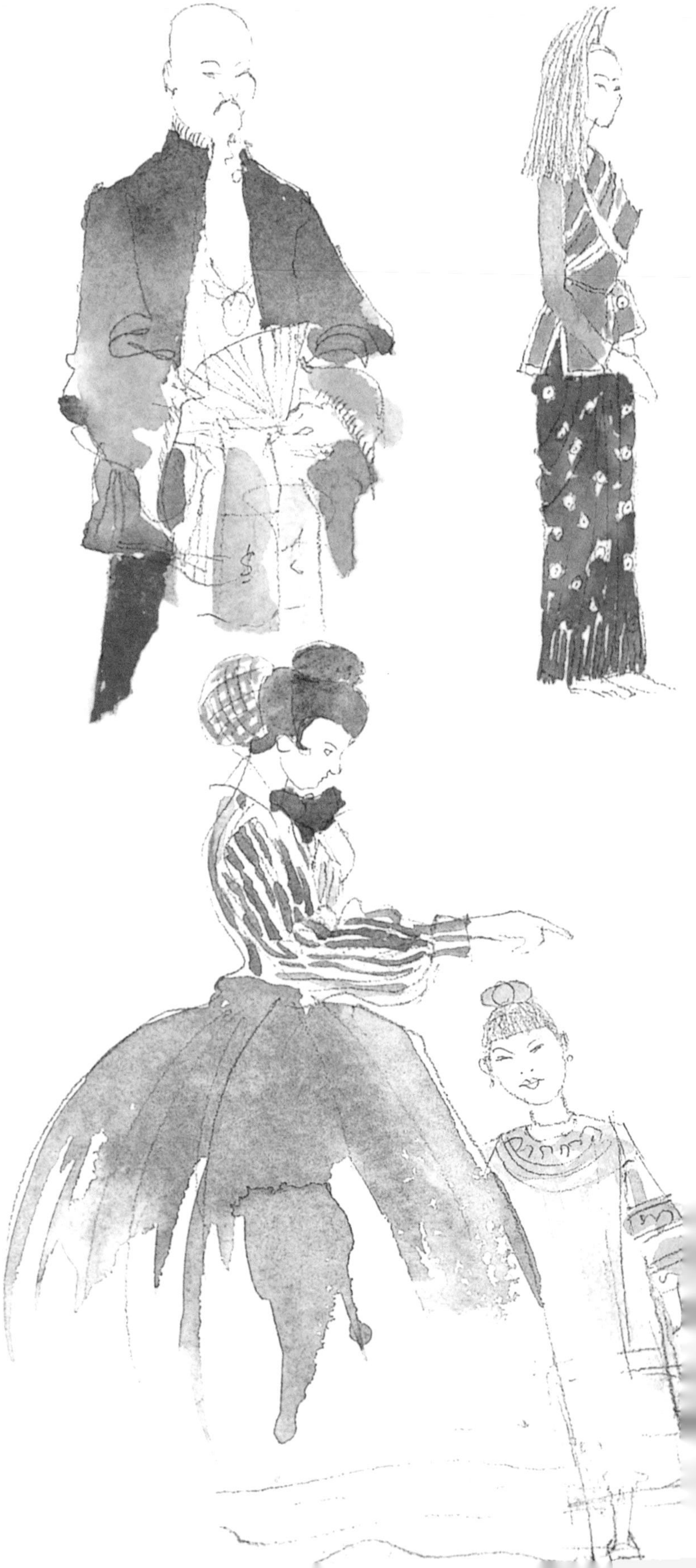

Still this did not signal the overnight birth of an industry. Thompson proceeded cautiously, at first operating out of his room at the Oriental where he continued to live. He could often be encountered in the lobby, an old-timer remembers, attracting guests with piles of shimmering silk casually draped over his arm and nearly always persuading them to buy some. The results increased his confidence, and soon there were enough orders to keep a number of weavers busier than they ever had been at their looms. In 1948, his silks were placed on sale at a souvenir shop that also sold silk yarn to weavers. A year later he opened a shop of his own on lower Surawong Road, and in 1950 the operation was finally put on a more businesslike basis with the registration of the Thai Silk Company, Ltd.

A major sales boost came when he was asked to weave silks for the Broadway production of *The King and I.* Irene Sharaff, the costume designer, had already used some of his fabrics in an earlier musical, *Mike Todd's Peepshow*, which featured a song written by Thailand's King Bhumibol Adulyadej. *The King and I*, however, offered a much more dazzling showcase. For this, Thompson not only produced a wide range of silks but also old photographs of both Thai and European dress dating from the period. The great success of the

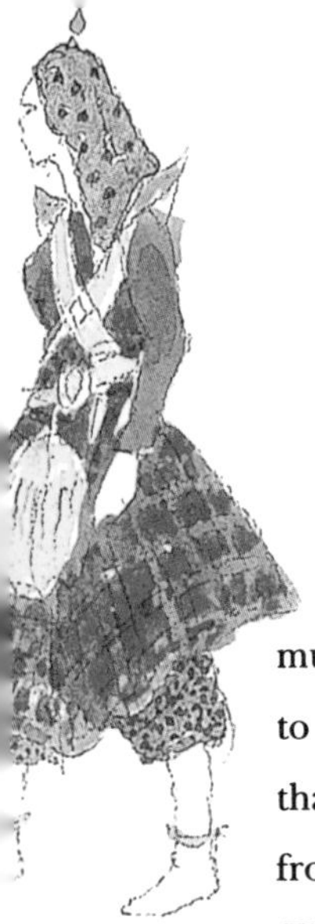

musical, as well as that of the later film, led to a flood of orders to Thompson's company and also to other companies who by that time were getting organized. Exports of Thai silk jumped from around half a million baht in 1950 (the year before *The King and I*) to nearly two million in 1952.

Opening a World Market

In retrospect, it can be seen that Thompson's most enduring contributions to Thai silk lay in two related areas: improvement of the product itself and the creation of a world market. The first was essential to the second. Weavers had to accustom themselves to the flying shuttle rather than the old time-consuming method of passing the thread from one side of the loom to the other by hand; only by doing so could production be increased and standard widths supplied to customers. Moreover, color-fast chemical dyes had to be substituted for the conventional vegetable ones, a delicate process that required considerable trial and error on the part of both Thompson and the weavers. When the proper color combination was achieved, the formula had to be carefully recorded so that it could be repeated without variation in subsequent orders. Finally, standards had to be rigorously maintained, a difficult task in any cottage industry and particularly so in one that had for so long produced only individual pieces.

Without a market, however, all these improvements would have been useless. Here, Thompson's success was due to a

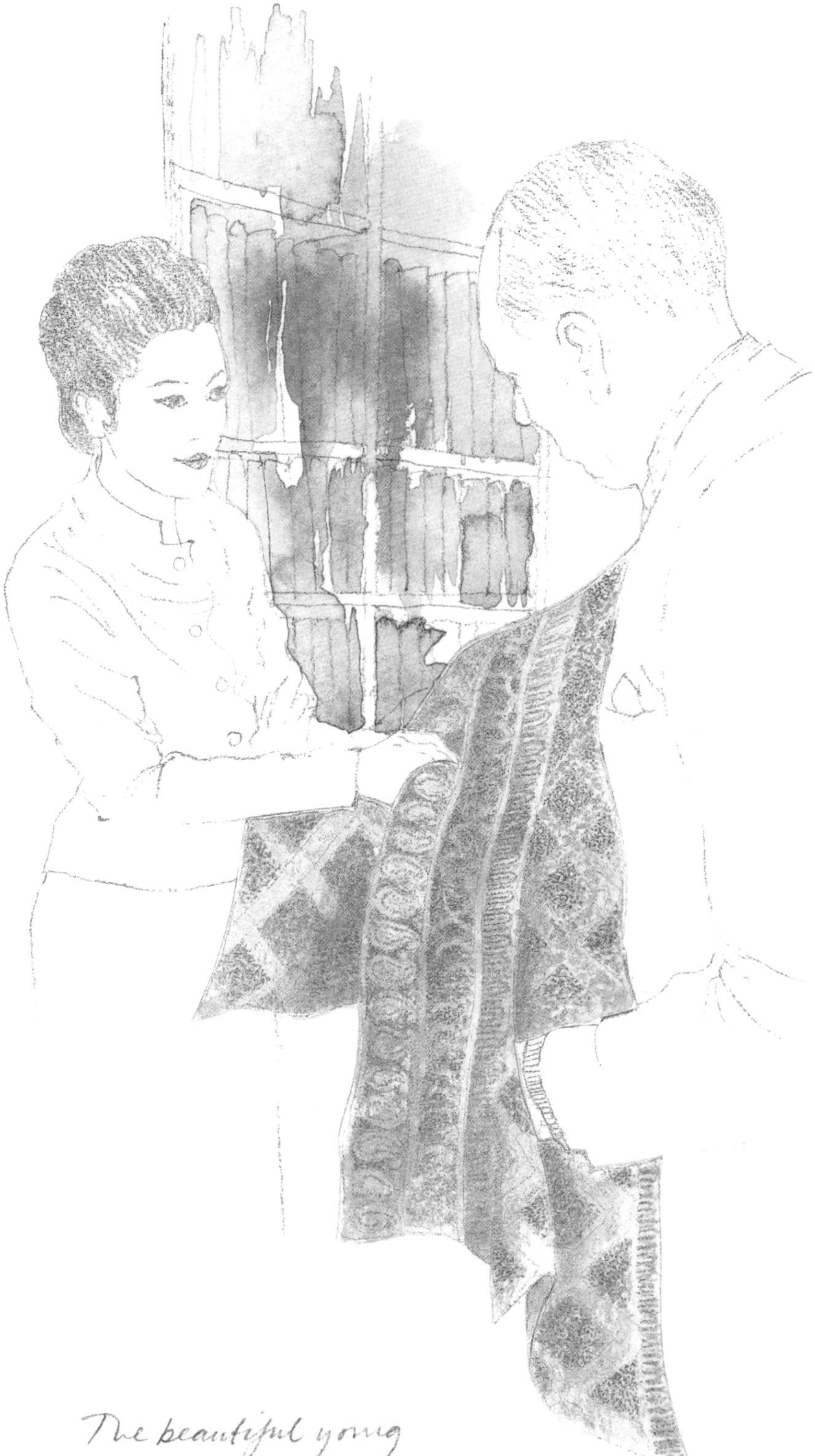

The beautiful young Queen of Thailand was one of the earliest patrons of Jim Thompson's silks.

Almost everyday, Jim Thompson crossed the klong outside his home to place orders with the silk weavers of Bangkrua.

combination of factors: contacts in some of the loftier social circles of the West, pure luck (as was the case in *The King and I*), and, perhaps most of all, personal charm and a singular flair for salesmanship that won over even the most doubtful customers.

Thailand's Most Famous Export

By the 1960s, silk had become Thailand's most famous export product, not only in brilliant solid colors but also in a wide range of prints (another area pioneered by Thompson) and a variety of weaves for home furnishings as well as fashion. Designers of the film *Ben Hur* chose Thompson silks for many of the principal costumes, and an English decorator used them in the Canaletto Room of Windsor Castle. The Woolworth heiress Barbara Hutton, an old friend, had special colors woven for her varied houses around the world. Thailand's beautiful Queen Sirikit was an early and loyal customer, and the dresses Pierre Balmain designed for a world tour she and the King made in 1959 brought the fabric new fame.

On Easter weekend in 1967, shortly after moving into handsome new offices in Bangkok, Jim Thompson went to the Cameron Highlands in northern Malaysia for a holiday with friends. On the last afternoon of his stay, while other members of the party were resting, he is presumed to have gone for a walk in the surrounding jungle; in any event, he was not there when the others came out for tea. An extensive search of the area that lasted several weeks revealed no trace of him, nor has any been found in the years since.

But the remarkable American left behind more than an enduring mystery. At the time of his disappearance, the company he founded was exporting a quarter of a million yards (230 kilometers) of silk a year and was buying the products of over five hundred looms. Many of these, it should be noted, were in the traditionally impoverished Northeast, not only providing a new livelihood for many families but also helping reduce the large-scale rural migration to cities like Bangkok. Nor was the company alone in the field: by the mid-1960s there were nearly a hundred firms, large and small, involved in either producing or selling silk and employing thousands of Thais.

For Jim Thompson, who had once described himself in a letter to his sister as being "like a missionary but with better visual results," it was the sort of legacy he would have wanted.

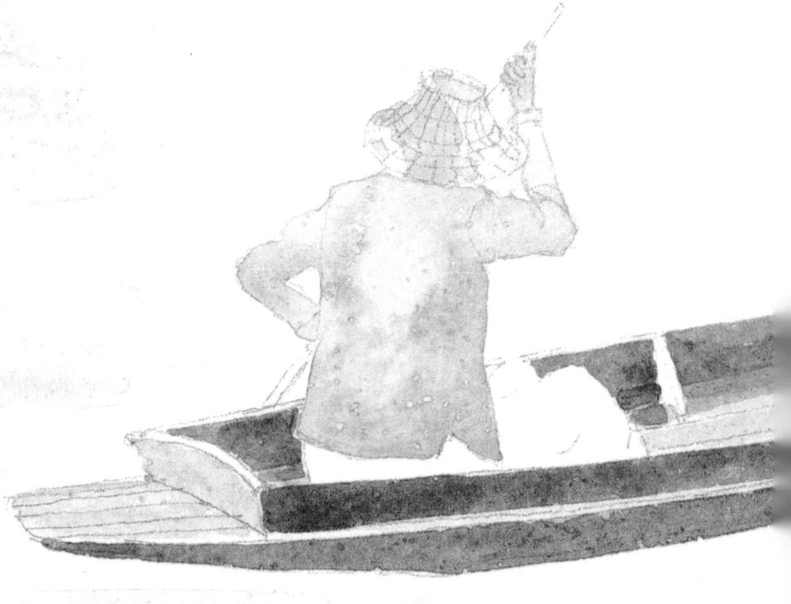

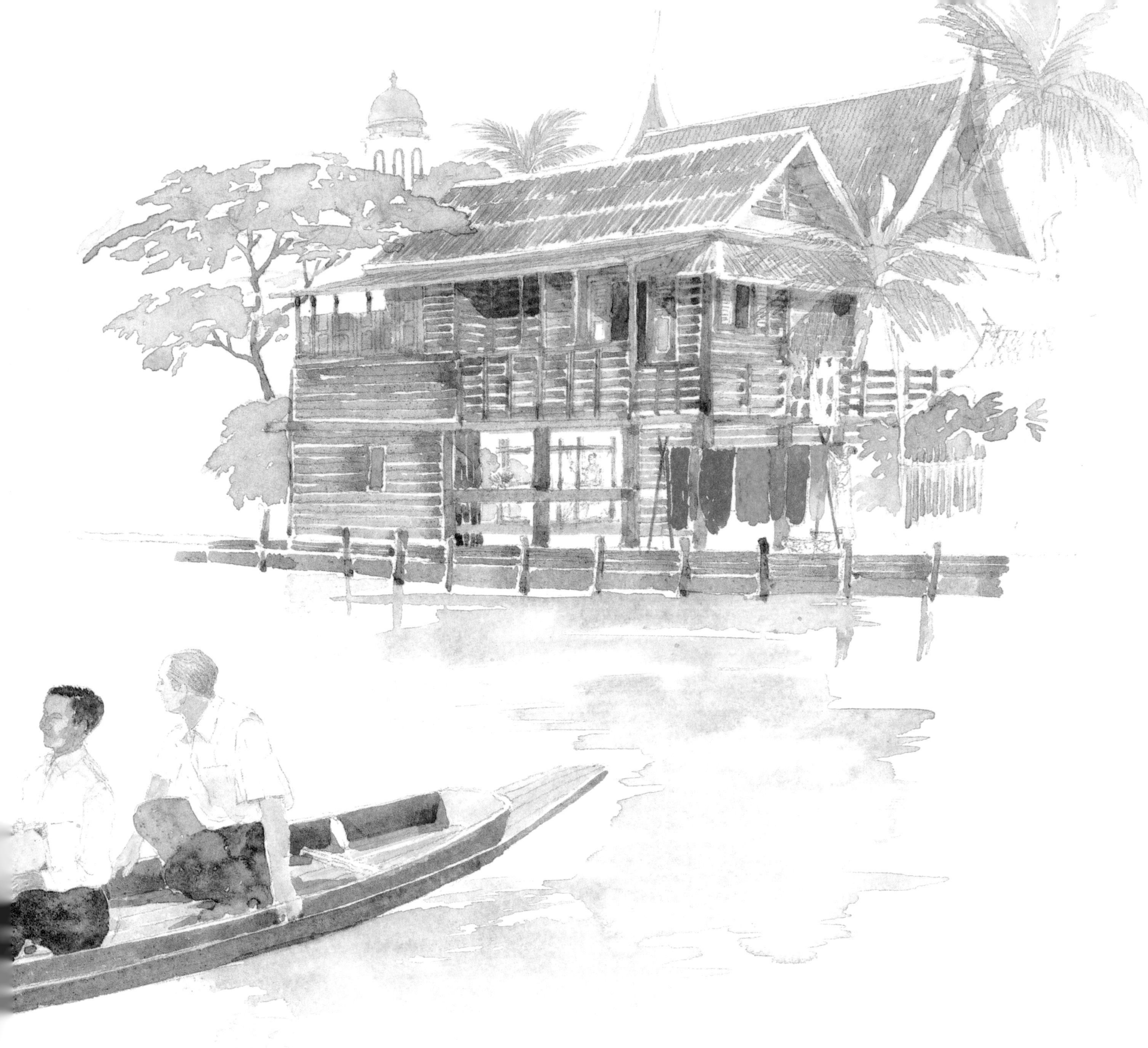

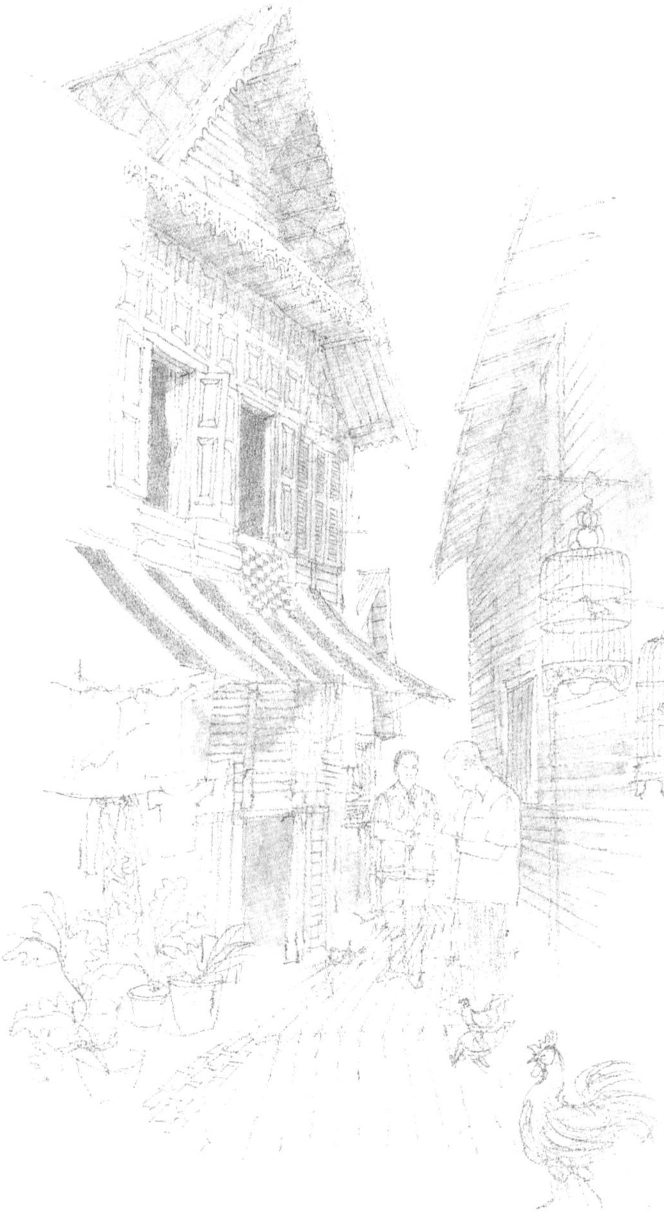

Along the boardwalks of Bangksue, Jim Thompson paid regular visits to a community of weavers who produced silks for his company.

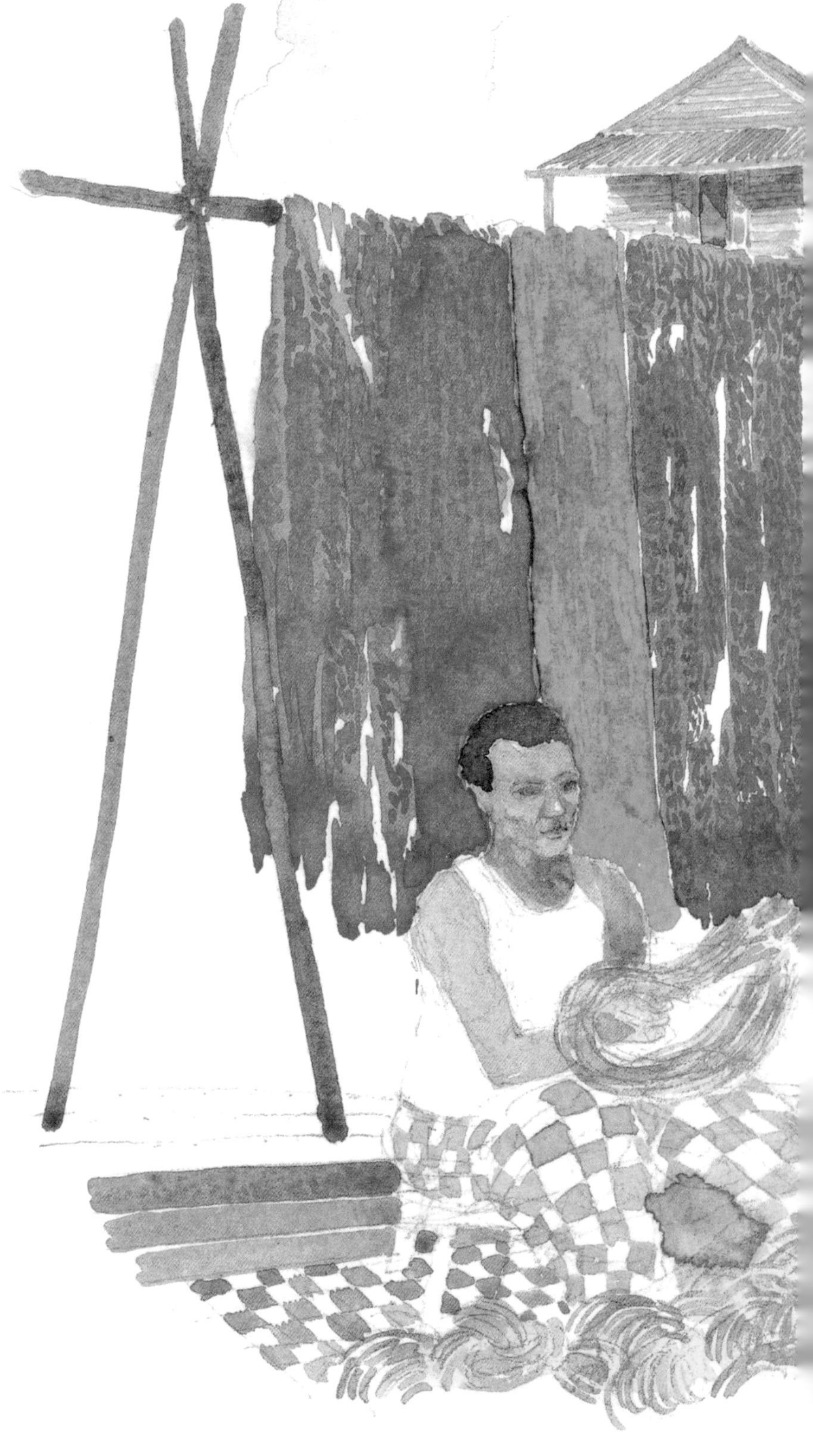

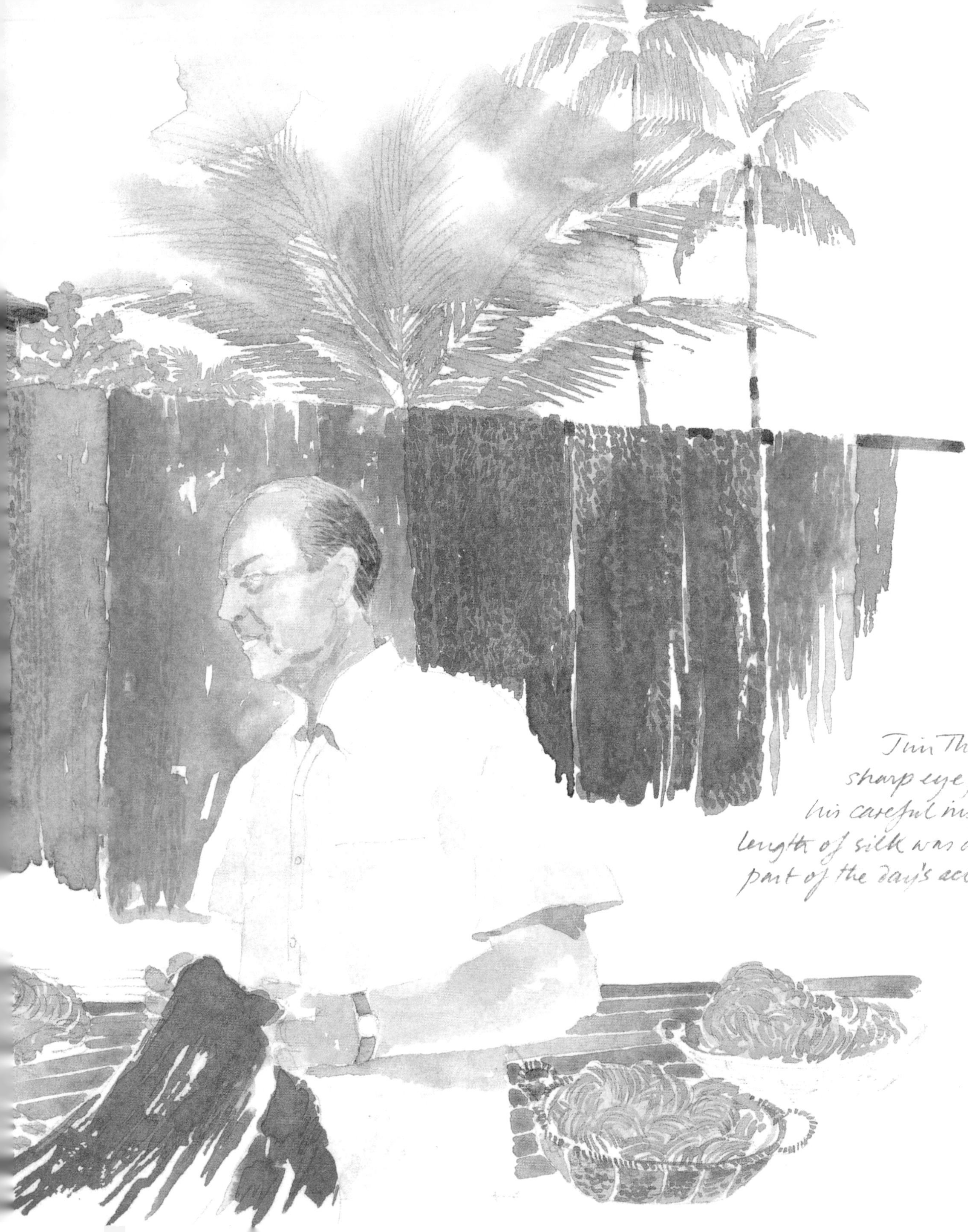

Jim Thompson had a sharp eye for detail, and his careful inspection of each length of silk was an important part of the day's activities.

The House on the Klong

Silk is not the only achievement for which Jim Thompson is remembered. Countless visitors to Bangkok go to another one that perhaps meant equally much to him: the beautiful Thai-style house where he lived and displayed his remarkable collection of Asian art.

Like Thailand's temples, its traditional houses have steep roofs that seem to strain toward the sky and bargeboards that curve gracefully upward at the ends. In the Central Thai style the side walls lean slightly inward, increasing the sense of airy lightness, and they are often made of long-lasting teak and elegantly paneled. One of the most practical features of the houses is the fact that they are built in prefabricated sections, each section forming a wall, which are fitted together by skilled carpenters and hung on a frame of wooden pillars. If the owners decide to move, the walls can be taken down, neatly stacked on a barge, and floated down the nearest canal or river to a new location.

The Antique Collection

During his first decade in Thailand, Thompson lived in a variety of accommodations. He also acquired an increasingly large collection of art, mostly Thai but also Chinese, Khmer, and Burmese, gathered on regular visits to antique shops. By the late 1950s this collection was so extensive he decided it was time to

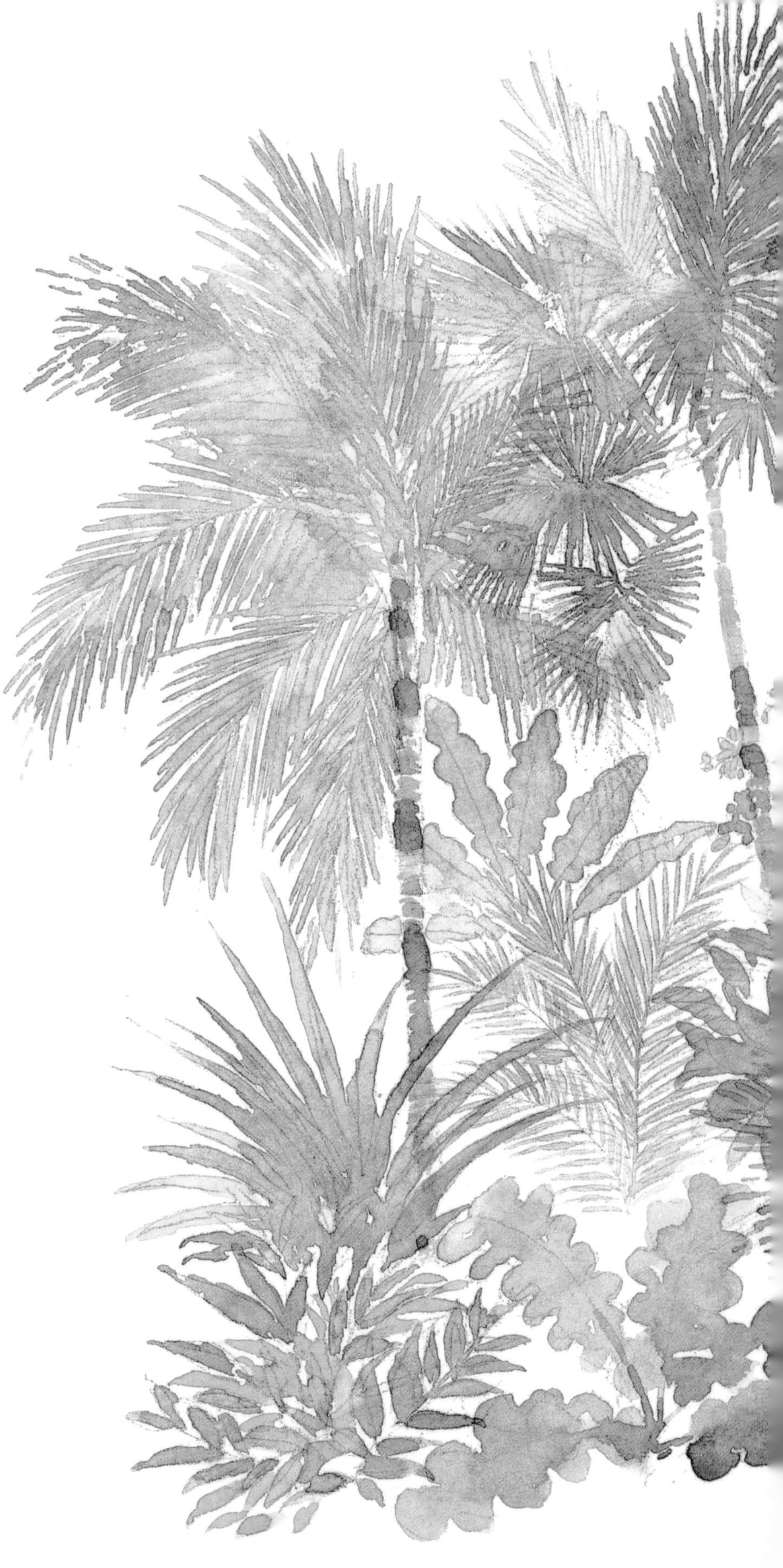

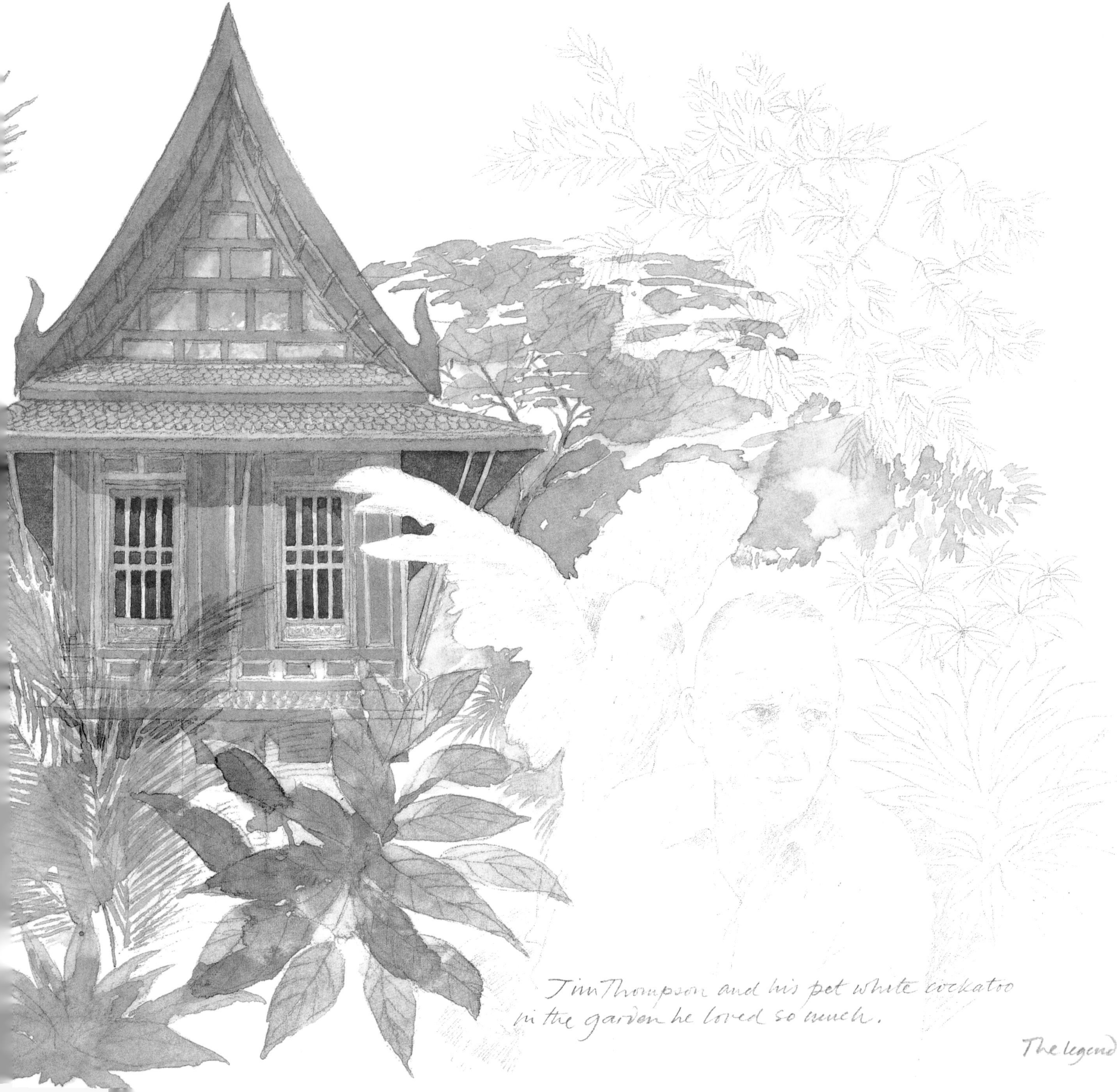

Jim Thompson and his pet white cockatoo in the garden he loved so much.

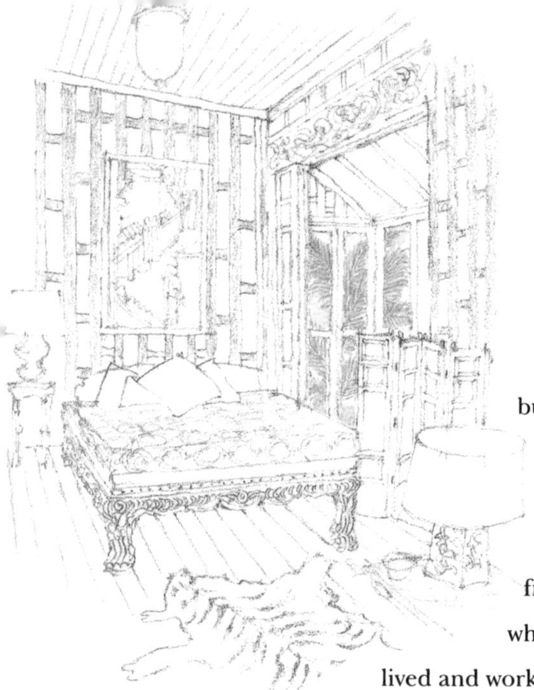

Jim Thompson's bedroom, with windows overlooking the klong and garden.

build a place that would provide a properly splendid setting for both the objects and his growing social life.

He chose a site across the canal from the community of Bangkrua, where many of his regular silk weavers lived and worked. The residence he eventually built was composed of all or parts of six separate buildings from a variety of locations. The one that was turned into his large drawing room came from Bangkrua, where five families had lived in it. Others were found in Ayutthaya, from which they were brought by river and canal. Construction took seven months and the completion ceremony was held on April 3, 1959.

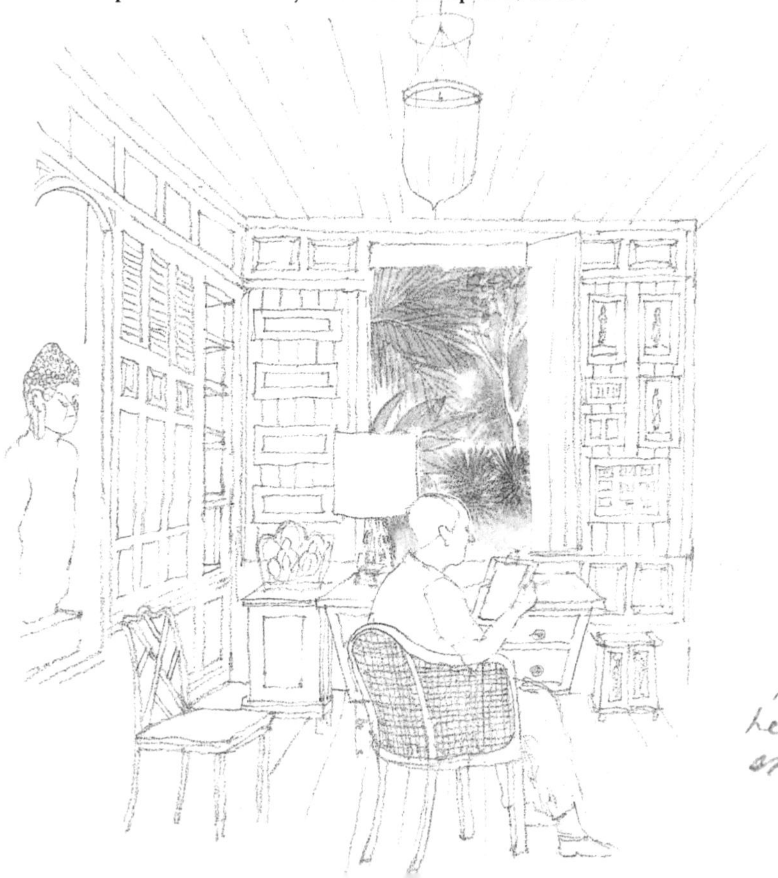

An air-conditioned study where he often did research on his extensive art collection.

Here the art collection could be displayed to dramatic effect — old Thai paintings, ranging from small to tapestry size; a seated, Khmer-style Buddha perfectly framed in a doorway; Burmese figures looking down from niches; blue-and-white Chinese porcelains, as well as a multi-colored ware called *Bencharong* made in China with Thai designs. In the dining room was a Chinese-style gaming table, while at one end of the drawing room were elaborately carved doors that had once been the entrance to a Chinese pawnshop. And everywhere, on chairs and couches and beds, were the glowing silks that he had made world famous.

The Social Occasions

Over the next eight years, this rich setting served as a theater for some of Bangkok's most dazzling social functions. Almost every notable visitor came with an introduction to Thompson, and a remarkable number were honored with invitations. From a graveled courtyard, they entered what was, architecturally, the rear of the house to a lofty hall floored with black-and-white Italian marble from a 19th-century Bangkok palace. Drinks were served in the splendid drawing room and dinner, if the party was small, around the gaming table; larger parties were held under the raised house or on the terrace overlooking the canal. Thai music was sometimes provided, and Thompson often brought out his pet white cockatoo to perch on his shoulder and entertain the guests.

Jim Thompson was renowned for his dinner parties where he entertained visiting celebrities in his charming dining room, which still looks the same today, or on the breezy terrace outside.

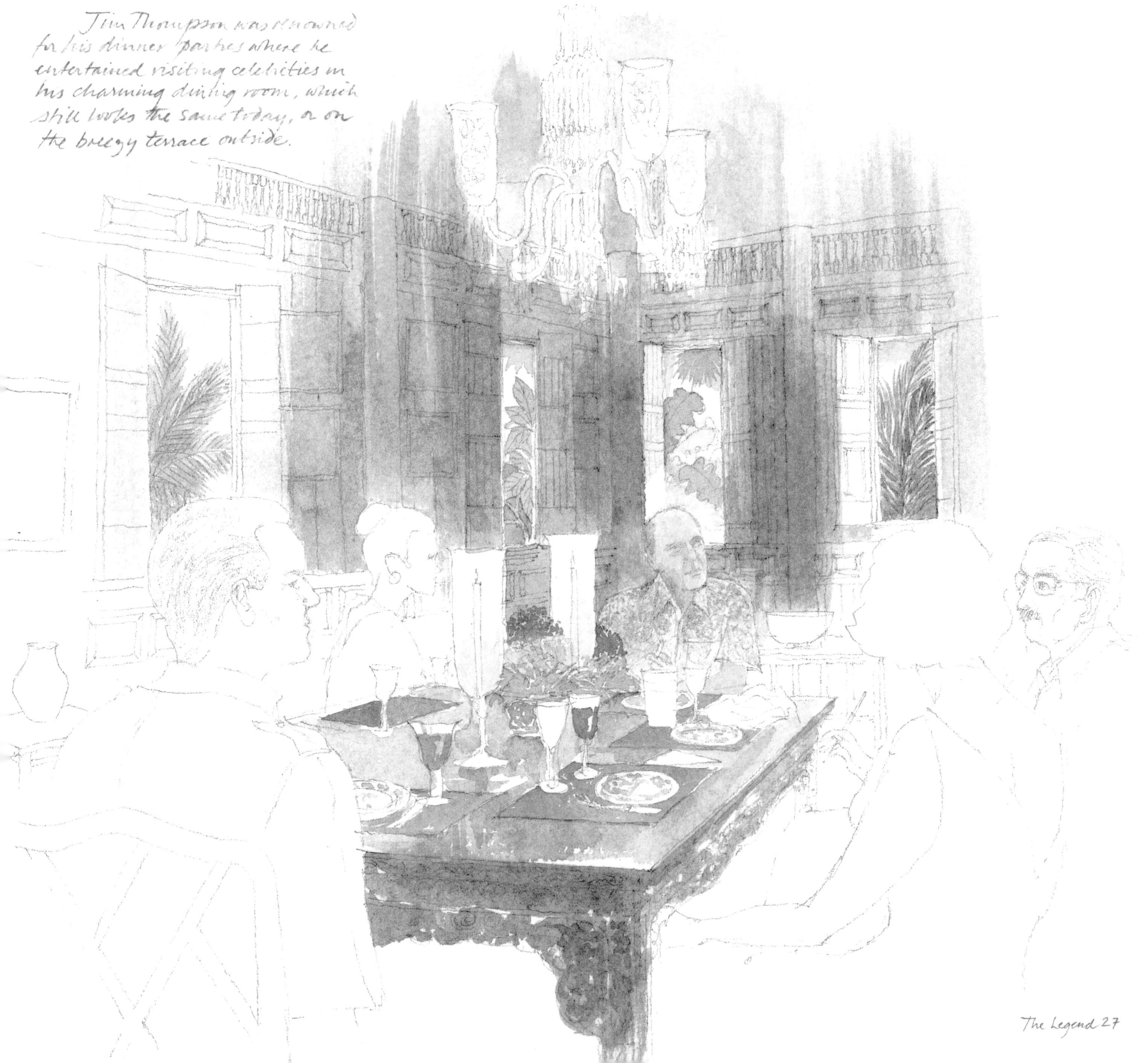

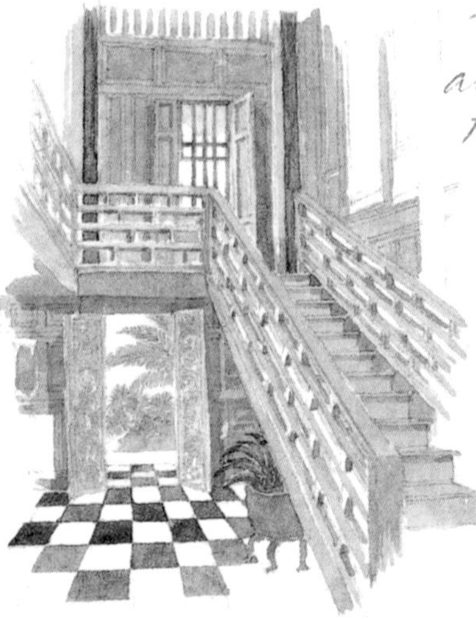

The entrance hall, tiled with black and white marble; guests ascended the stairs to the various rooms above.

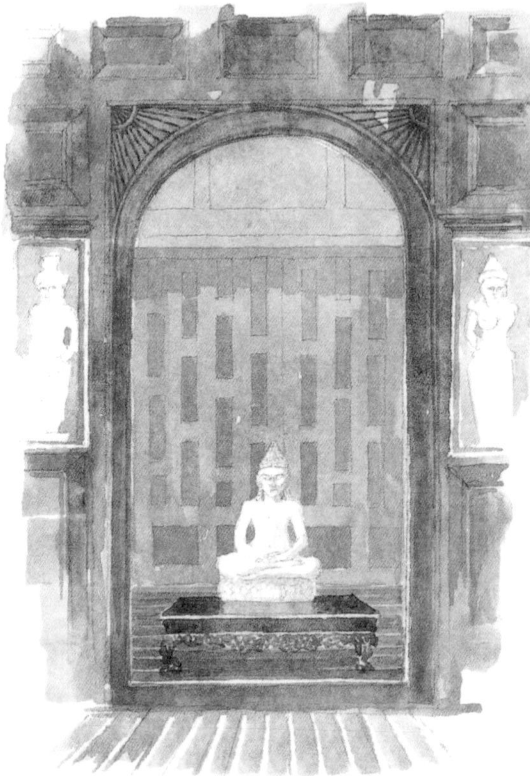

A Khmer-style seated Buddha image is exquisitely framed in an archway leading off the upper entrance hall.

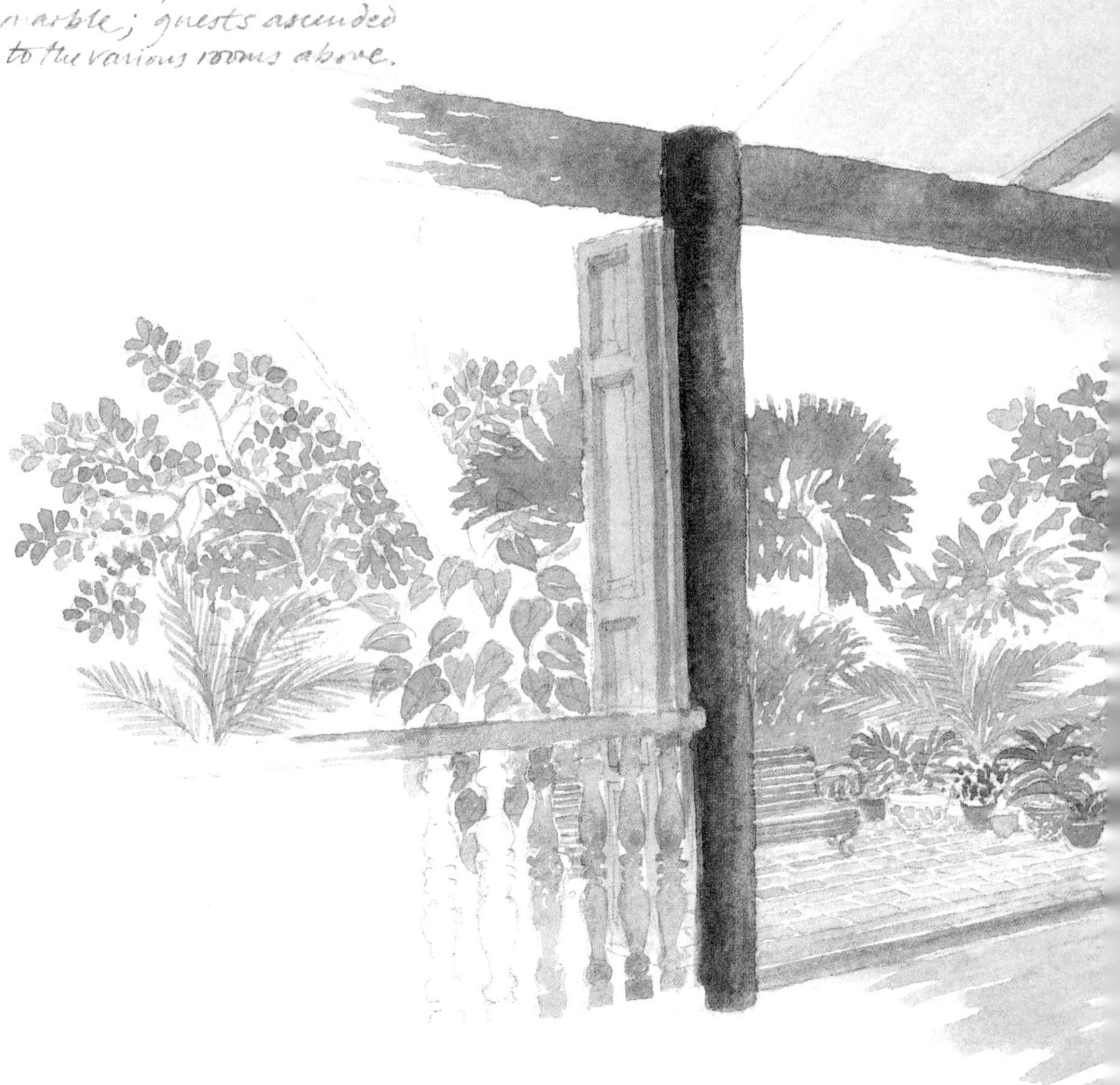

The spacious drawing room opens on one side to a terrace overlooking the Klong. Bold splashes of color are provided by silk cushions.

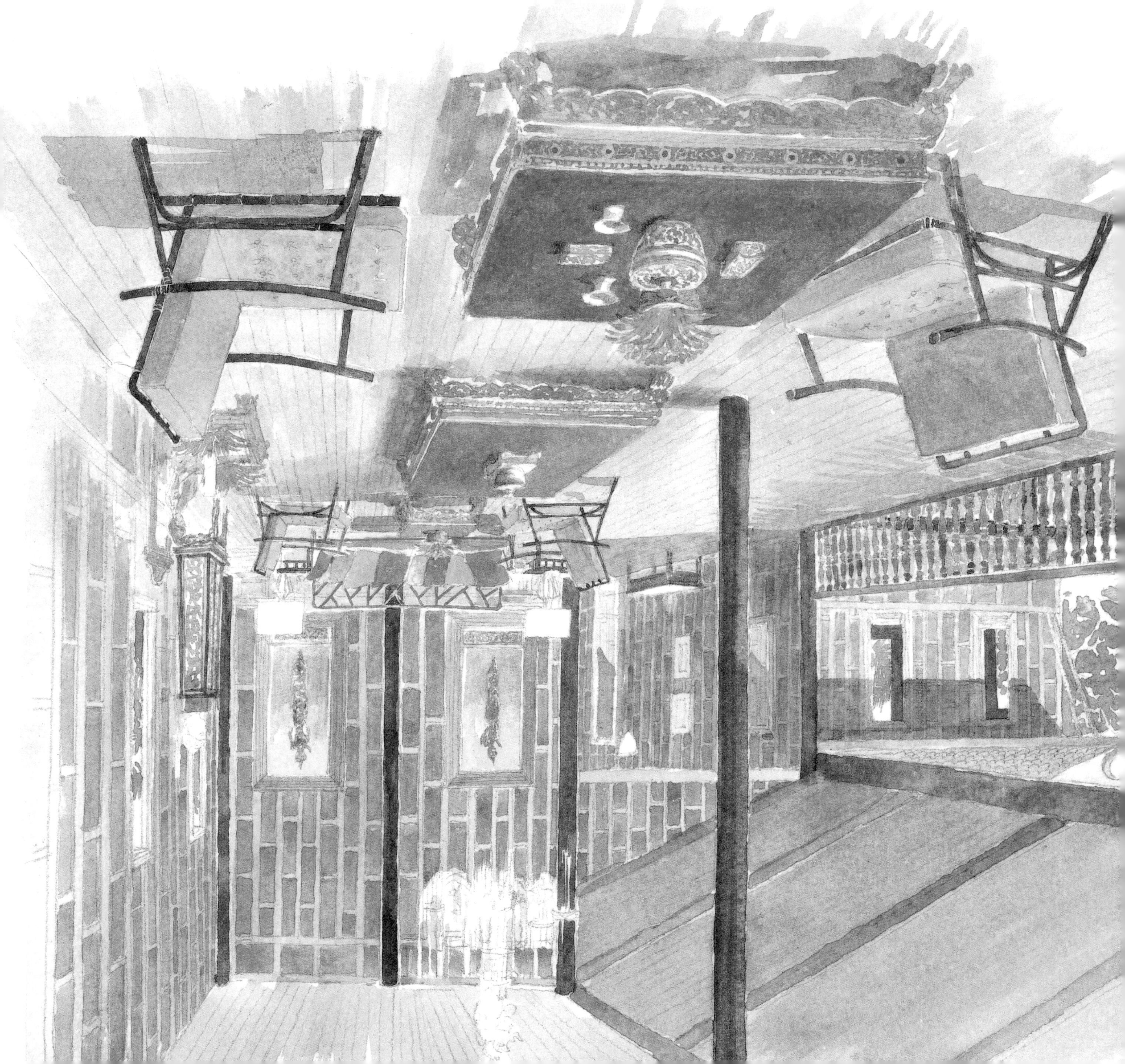

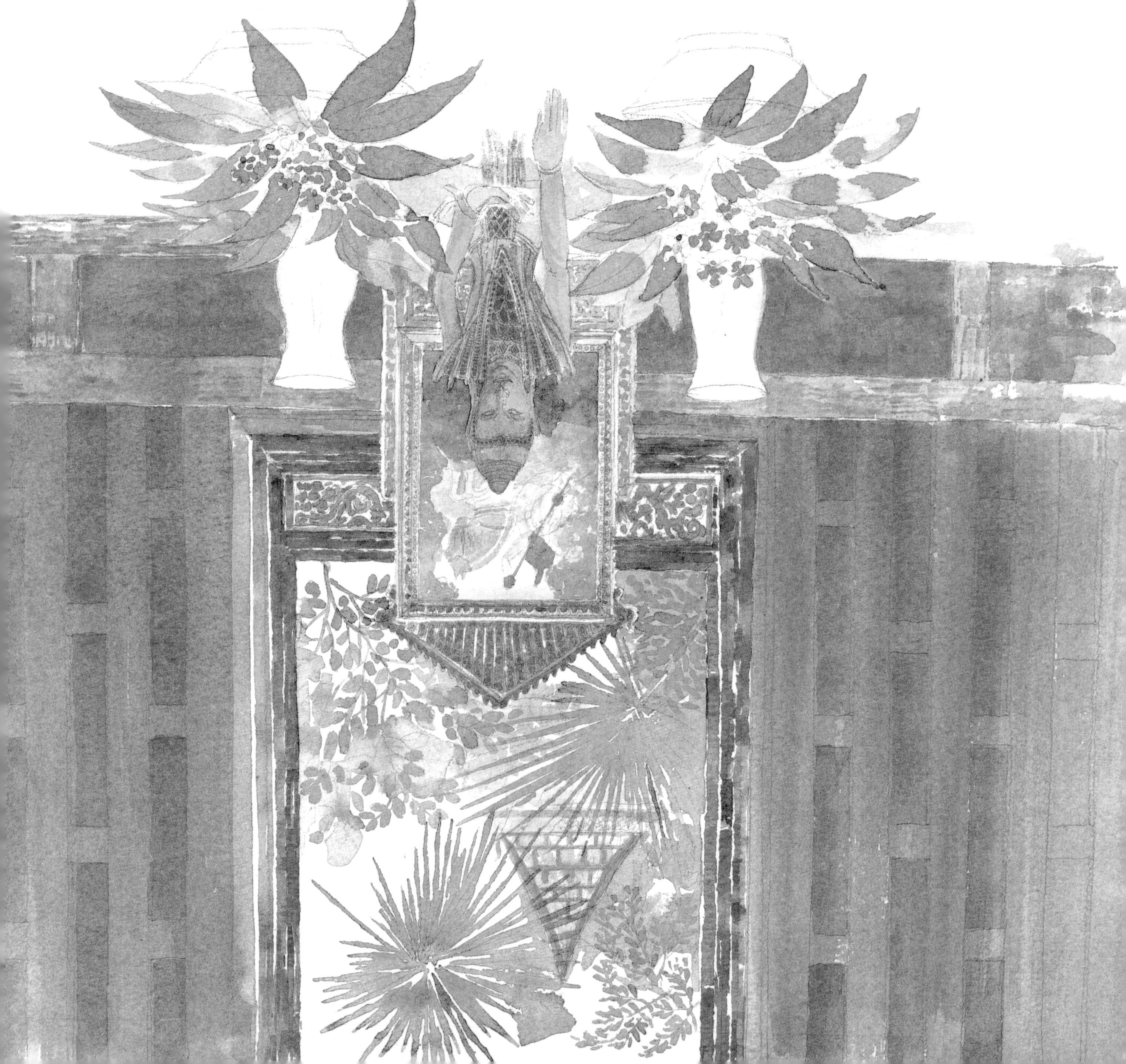

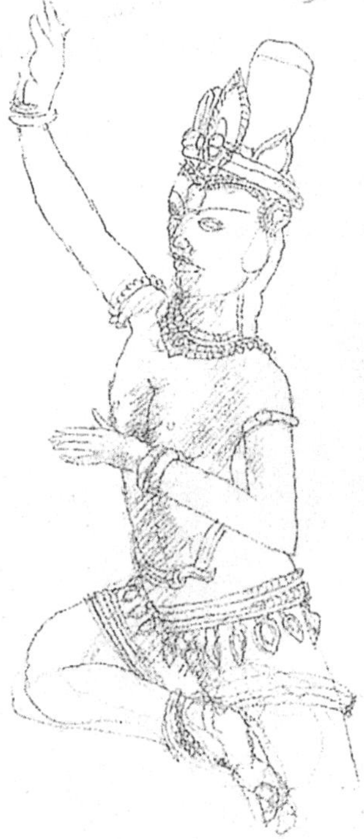

Dancing figure of Chanda-li, a Hindu deity.

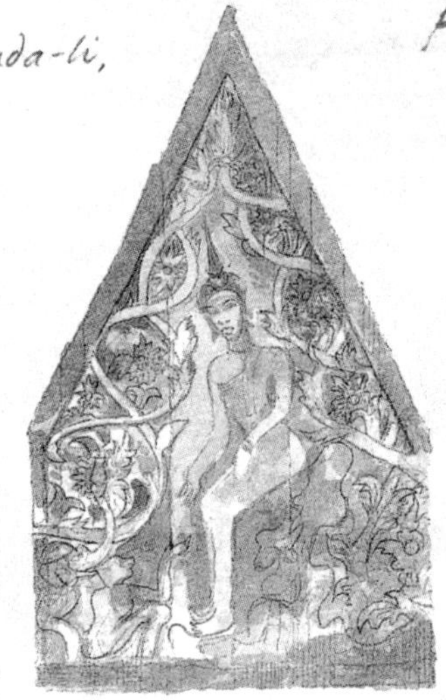

Wood carving showing a seated Buddha image.

Bencharong, a five-colored porcelain made in China for export to Thailand.

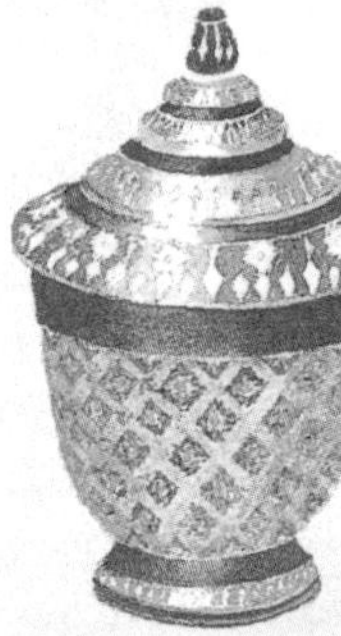

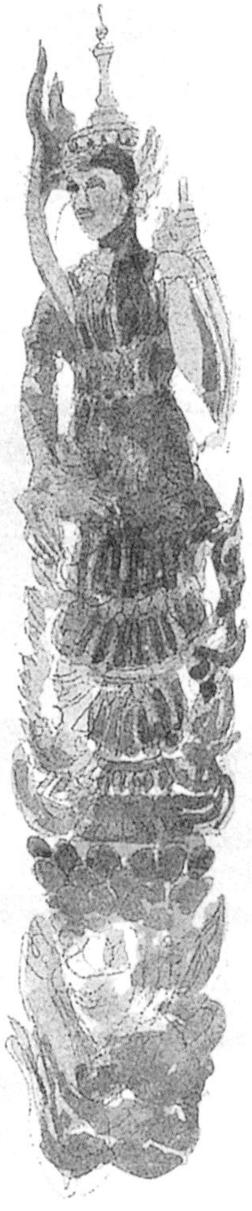

Carved wooden figure of a Burmese "nat," or spirit.

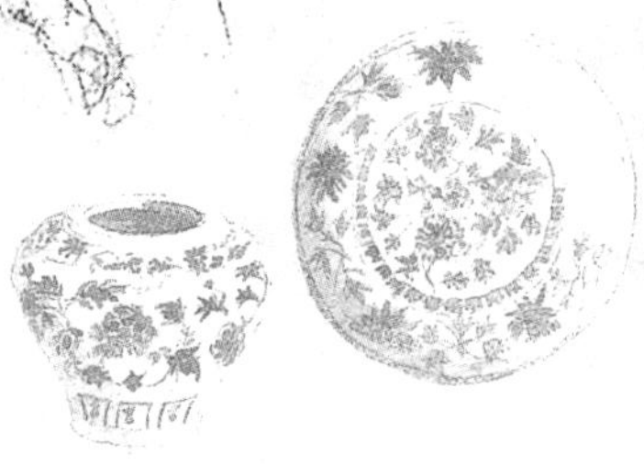

Ming Dynasty export porcelain

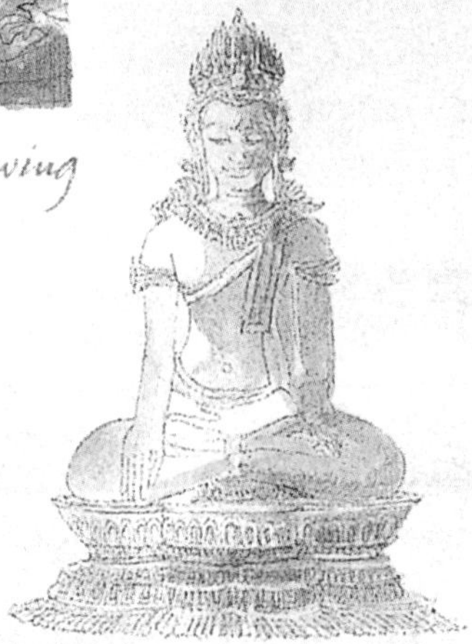

Seated Buddha image in the Lopburi-Khmer style

A gilded Burmese Buddha image stands
veen two old lamps below a window in the
ving room. Fresh flowers are arranged
ery day in the room, as they were when
im Thompson lived there.

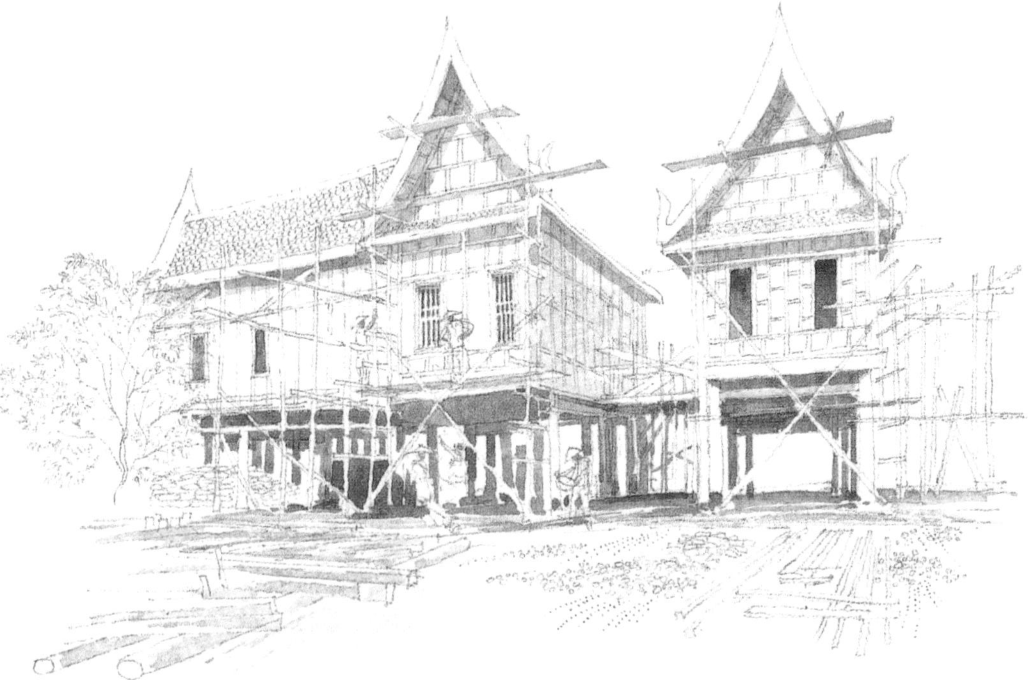

Trained as an architect in America, Jim Thompson paid daily visits to oversee the construction of the house.

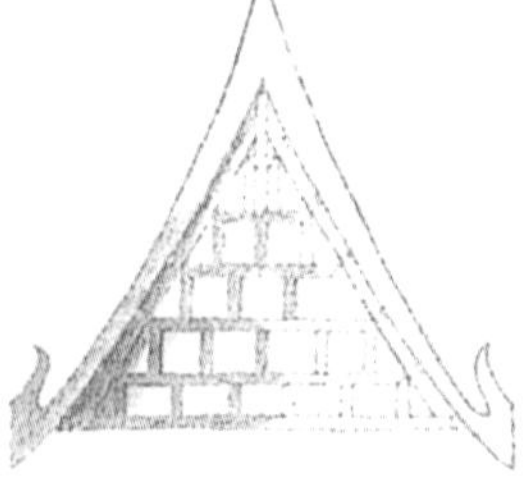

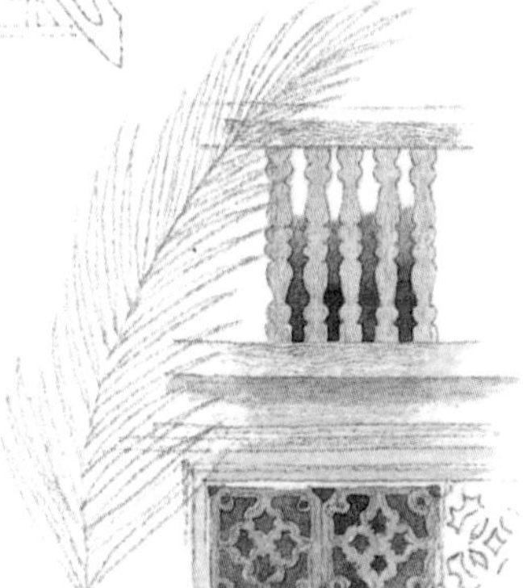

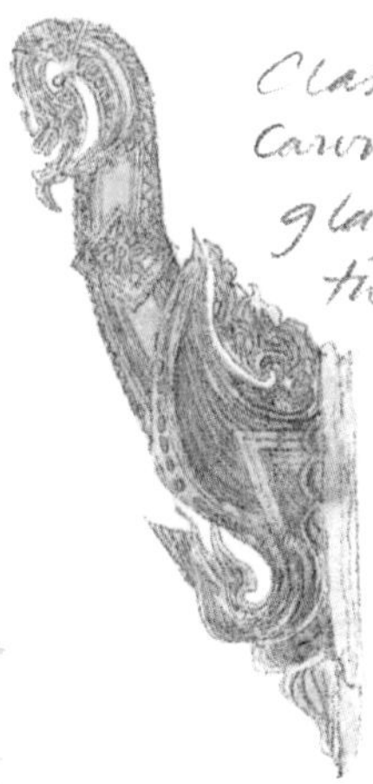

Classic Thai wood carvings and old glazed tiles adorn the house and are part of its visual appeal.

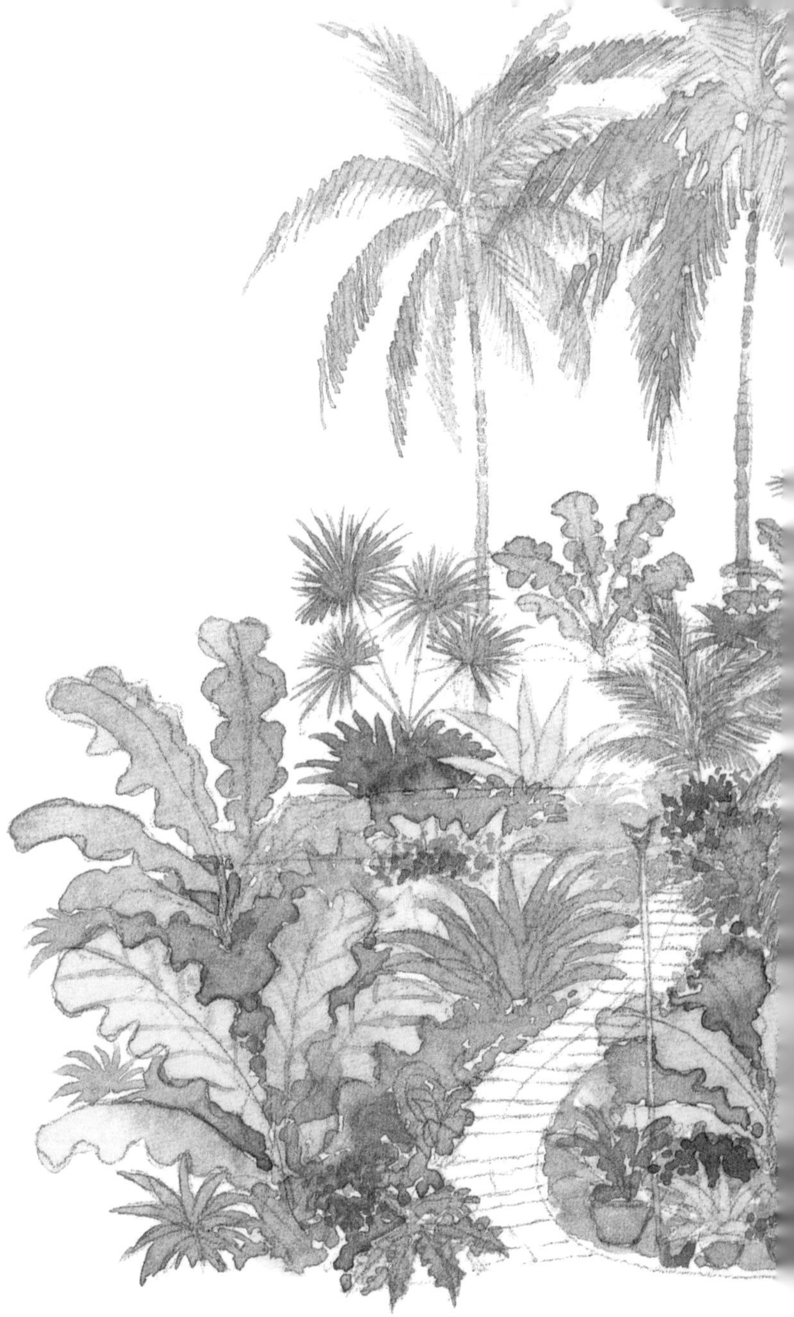

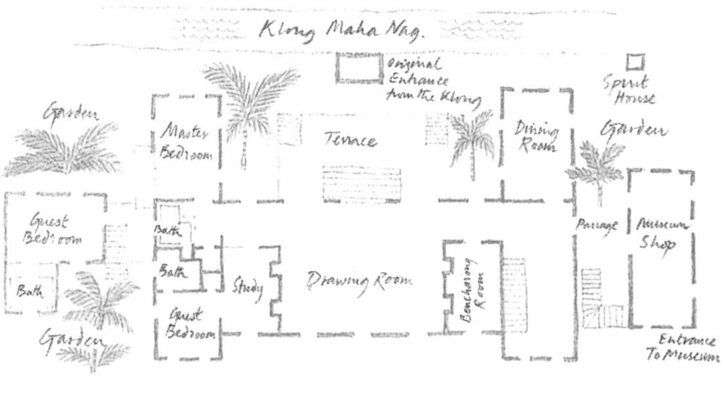

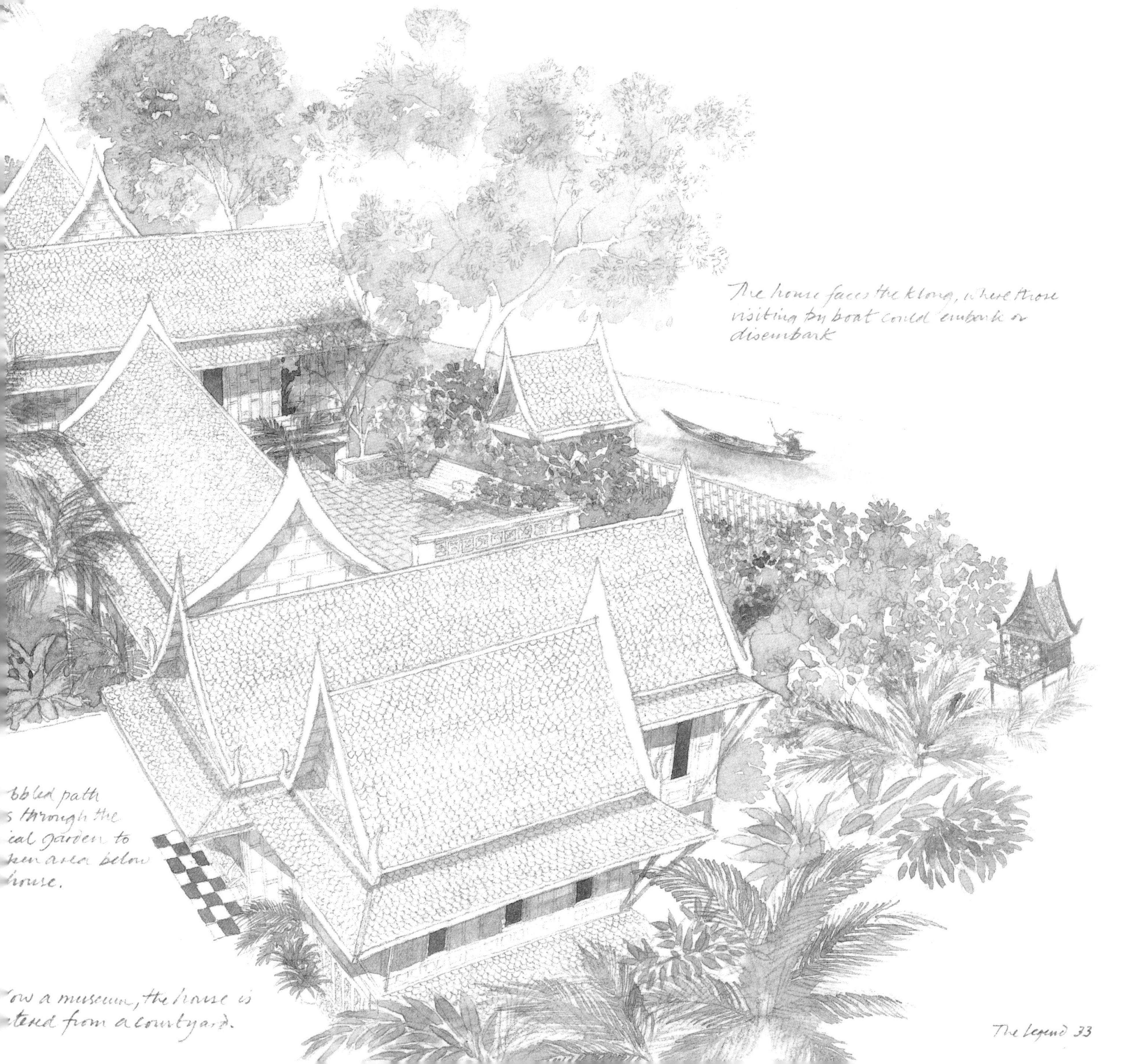
The house faces the klong, where those visiting by boat could embark or disembark
bbled path
s through the
ical garden to
hen area below
house.
ow a museum, the house is
tered from a courtyard.

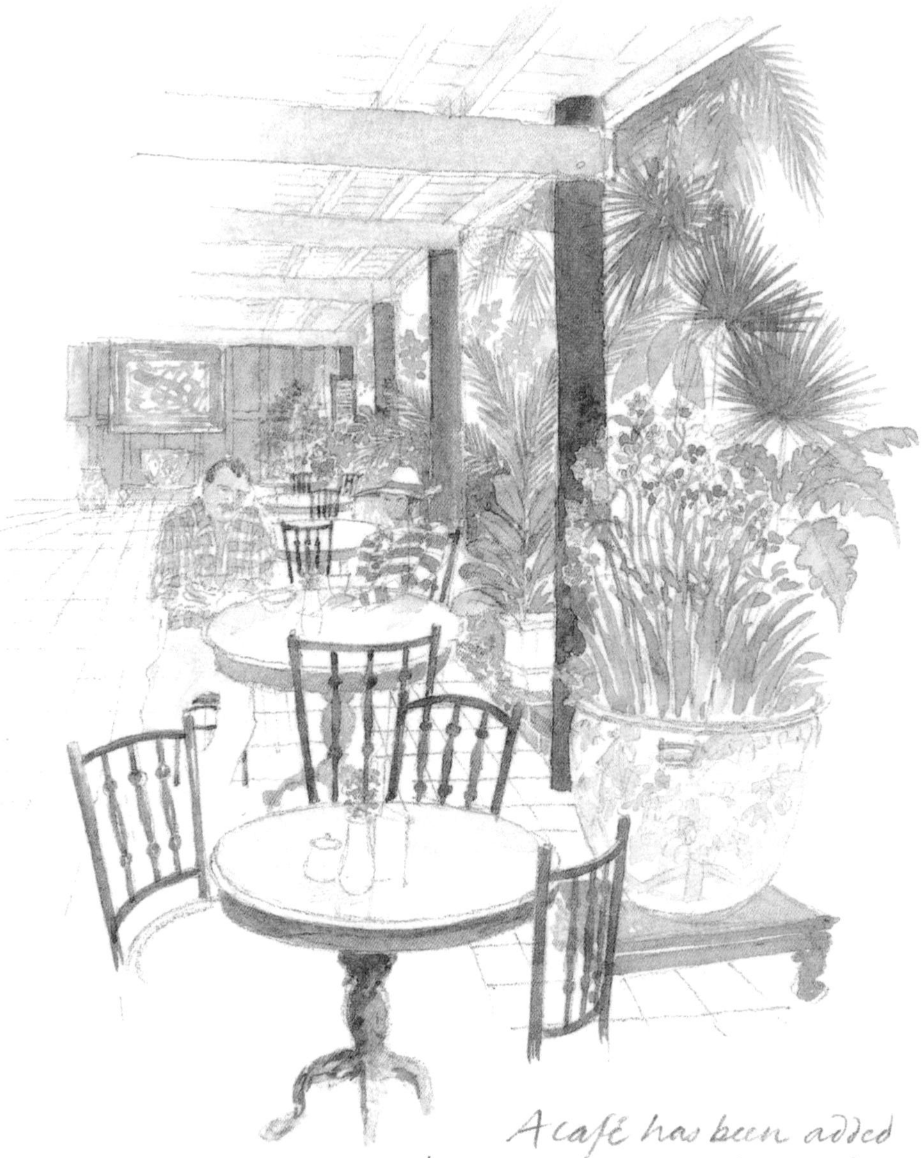

A café has been added to the open area beneath the house, which now offers refreshments to visitors.

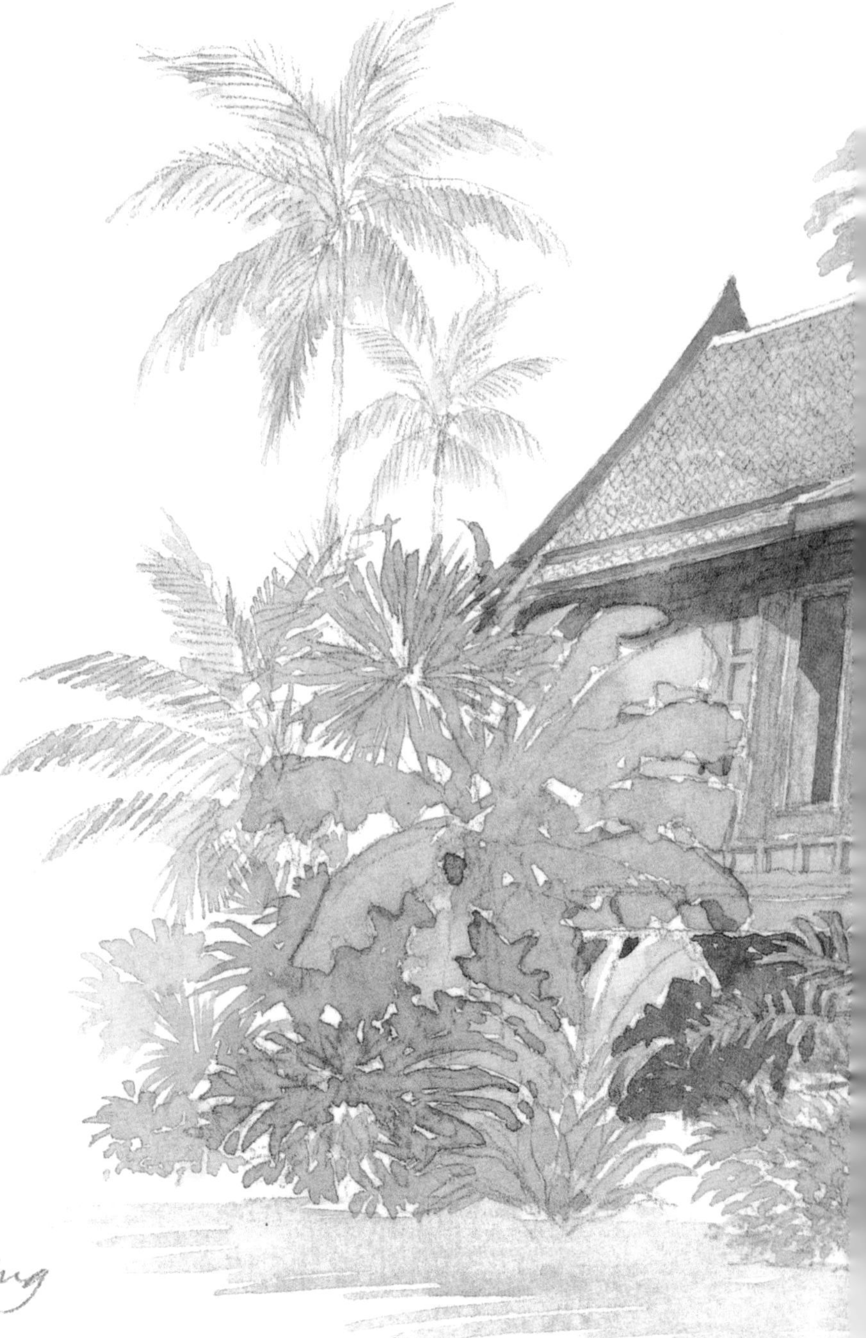

View of the house as seen from the courtyard surrounded by an ever-changing garden of tropical plants.

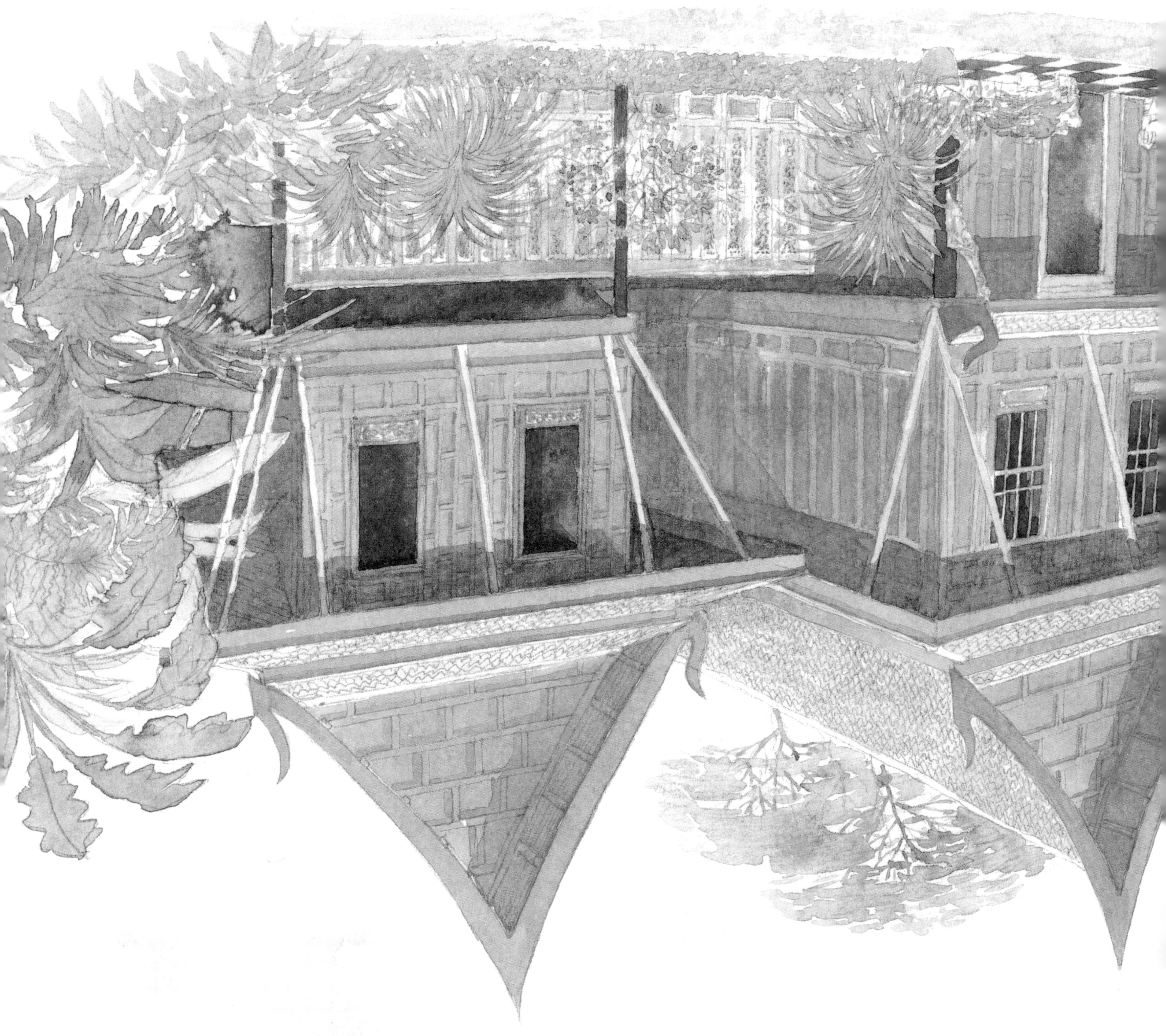

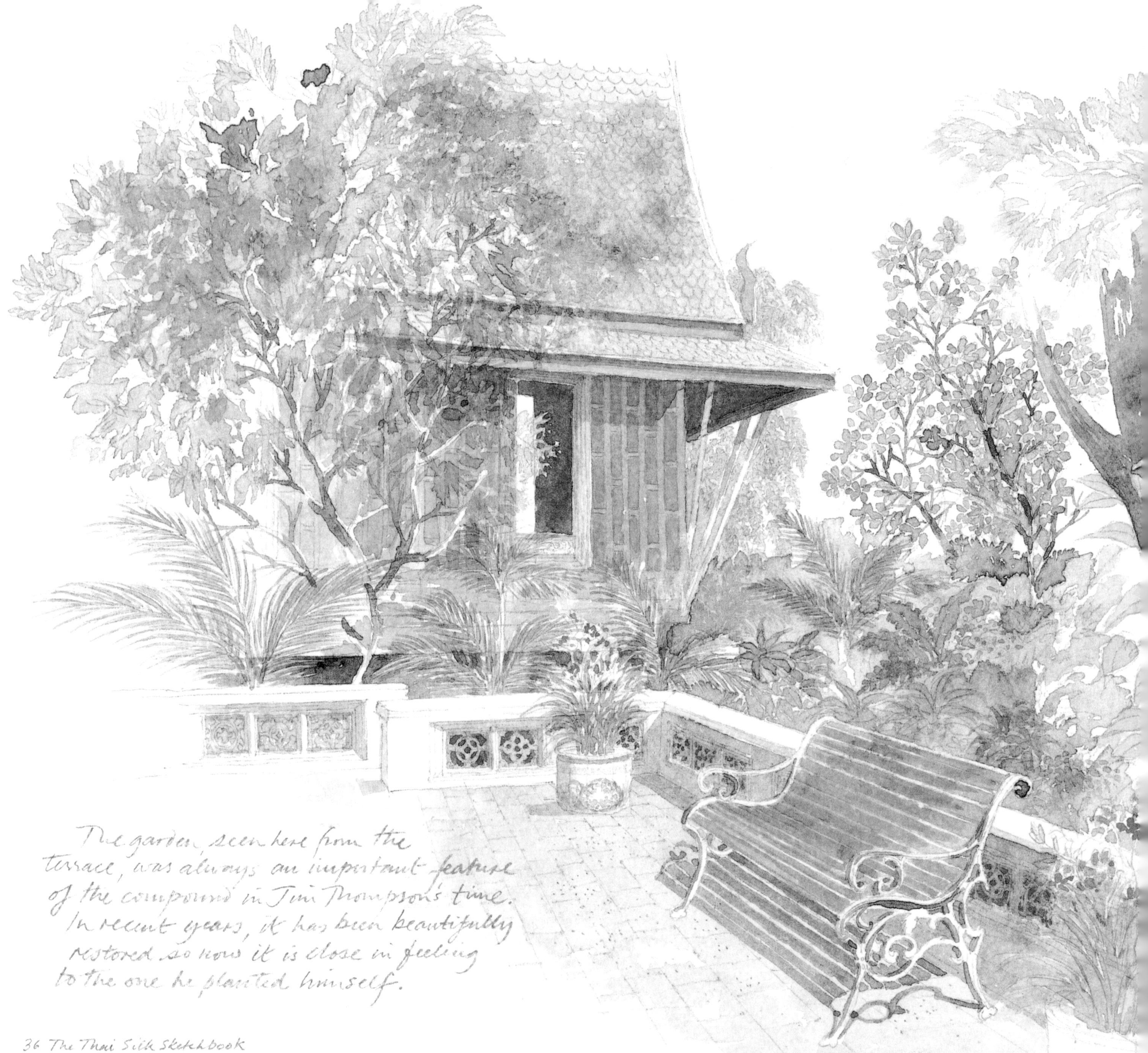

The garden, seen here from the terrace, was always an important feature of the compound in Jim Thompson's time. In recent years, it has been beautifully restored so now it is close in feeling to the one he planted himself.

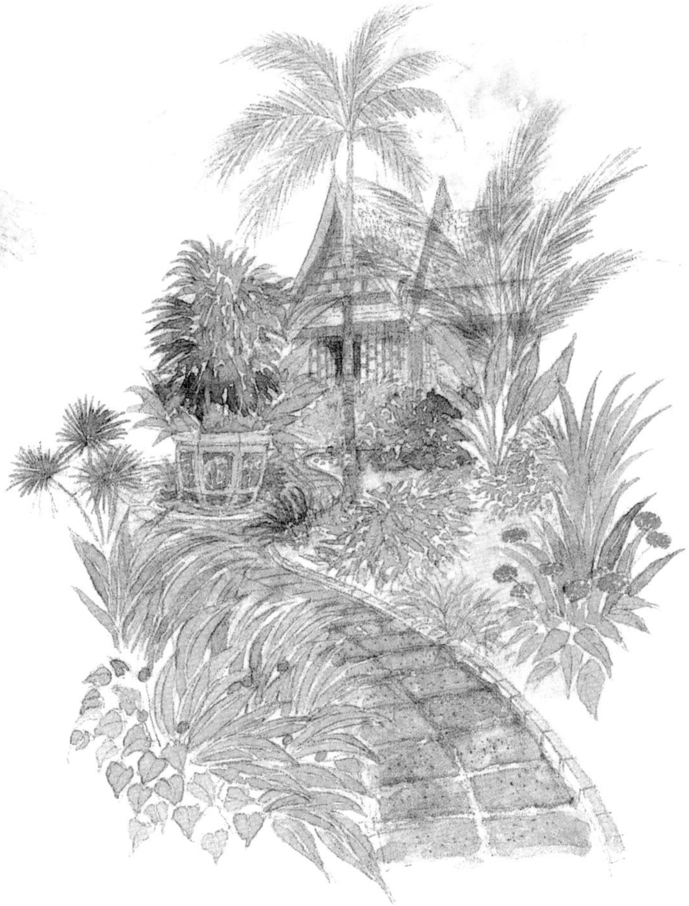

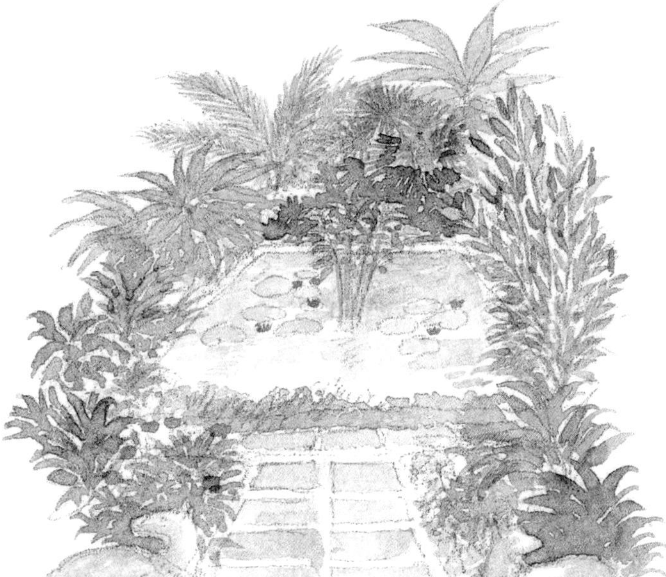

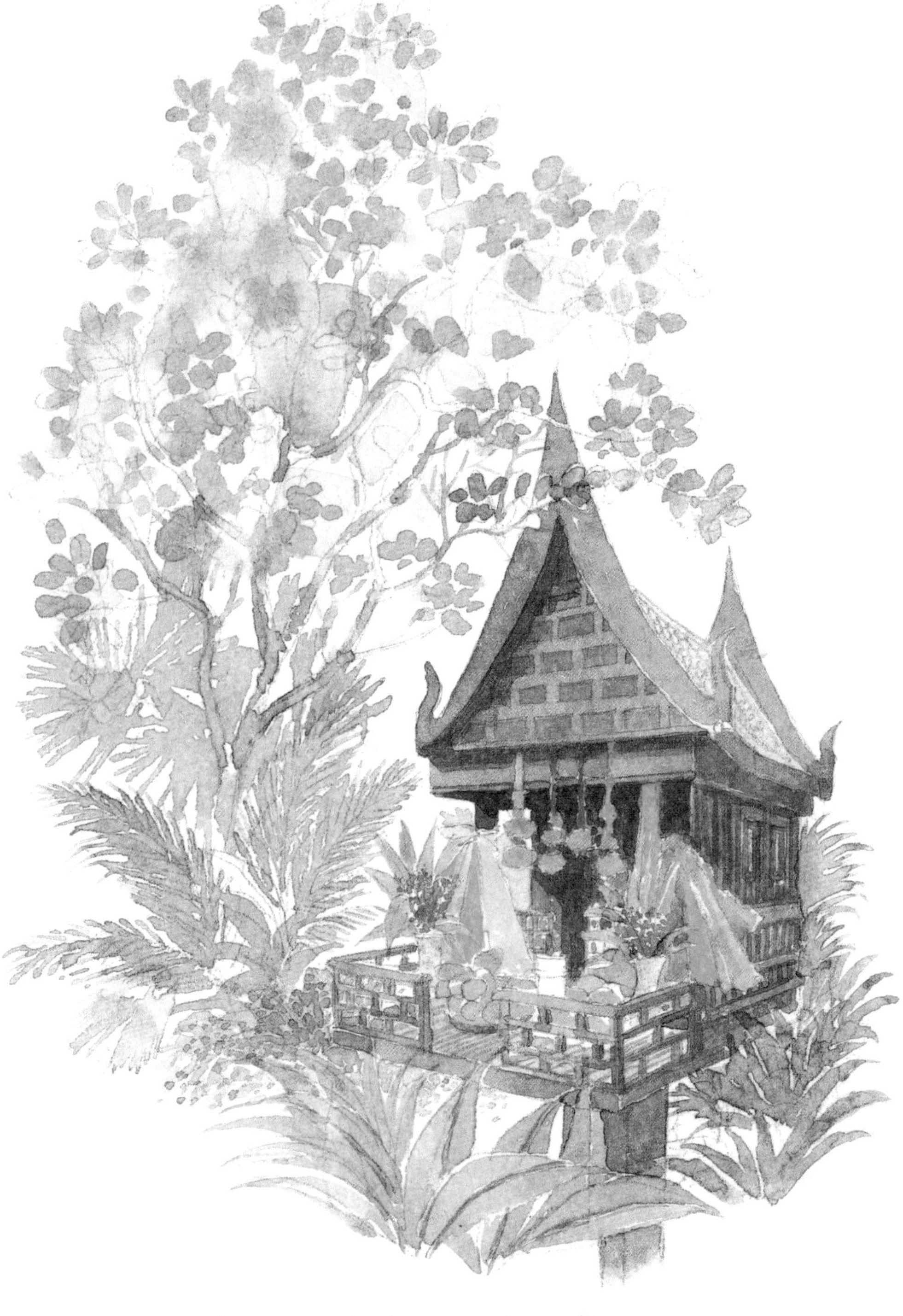

The spirit house, where the guardian spirit of the compound resides and where daily offerings are made.

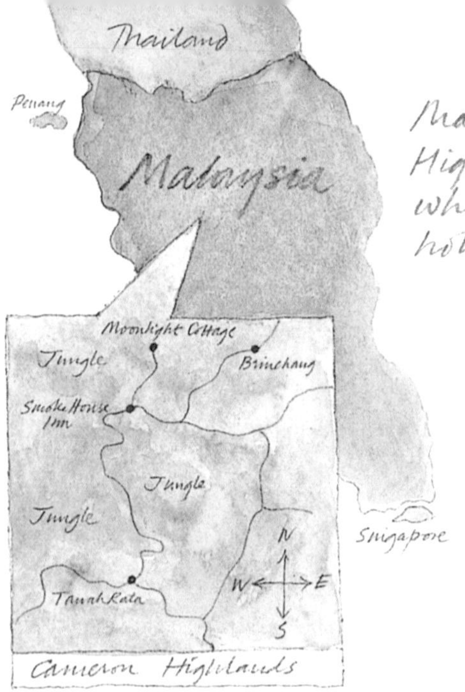

Map showing the Cameron Highlands in northern Malaysia, where Jim Thompson went for a holiday in 1967.

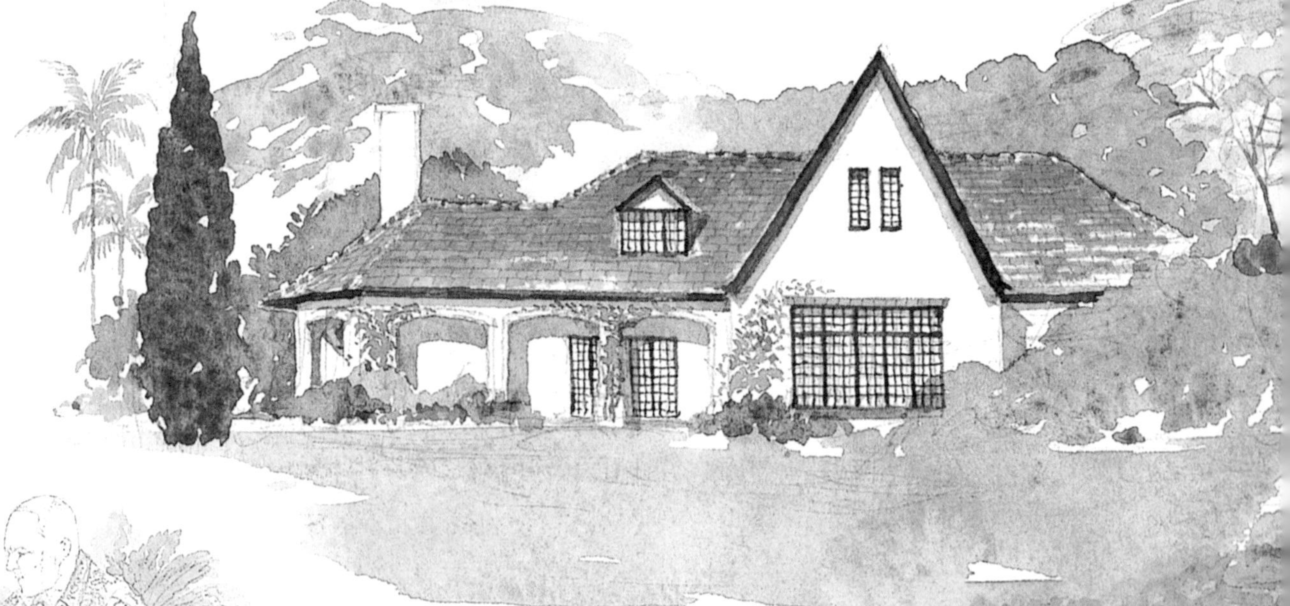

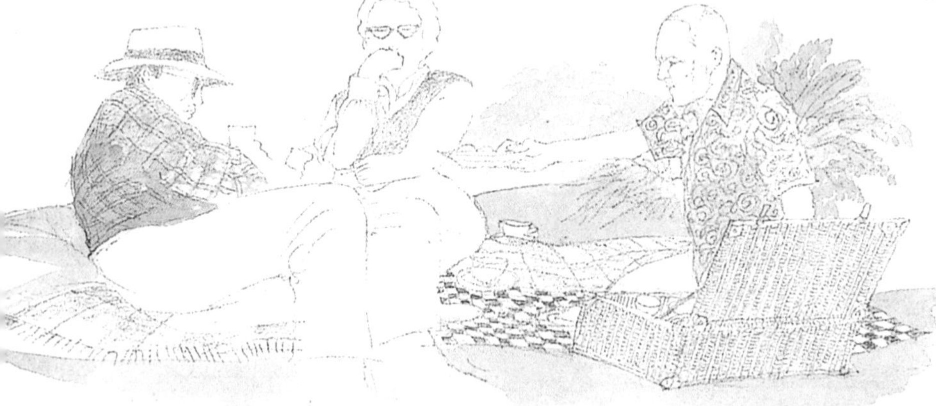

With his friends Dr. and Mrs T.G. Ling, Jim Thompson enjoyed a picnic on Easter Sunday afternoon.

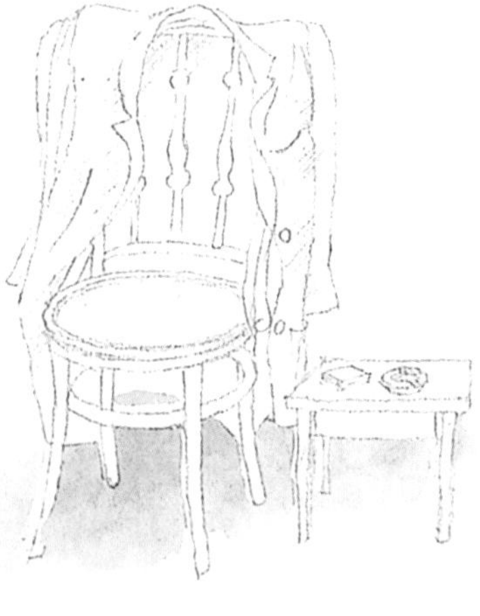

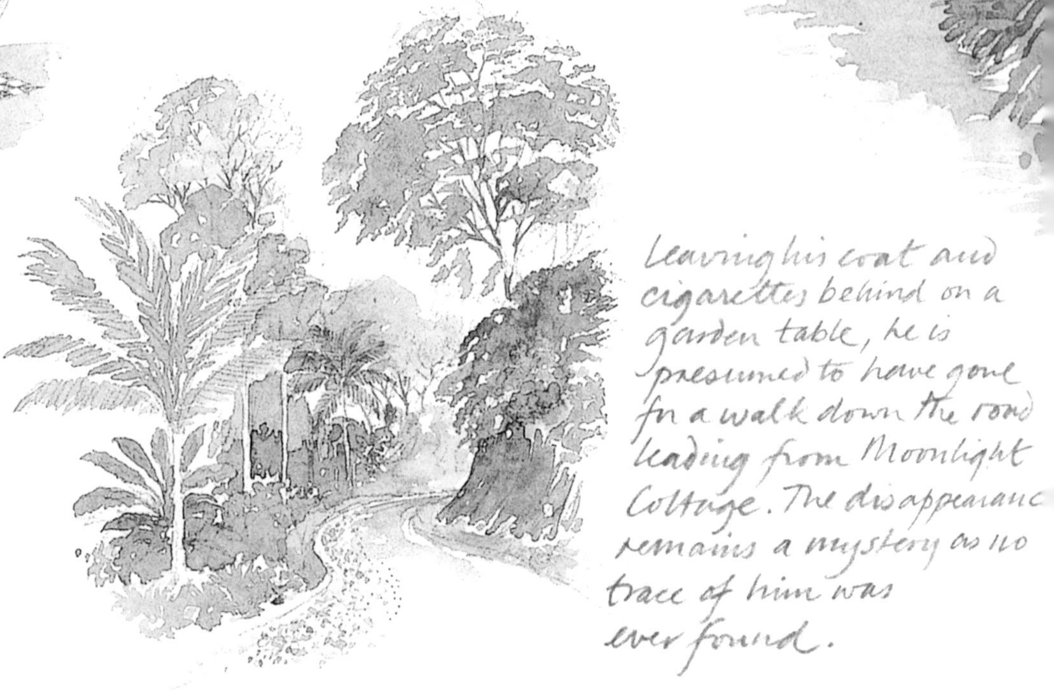

Leaving his coat and cigarettes behind on a garden table, he is presumed to have gone for a walk down the road leading from Moonlight Cottage. The disappearance remains a mystery as no trace of him was ever found.

Moonlight Cottage, the hilltop house of friends where he stayed. The surrounding jungle, at the time, was some of the densest in the world.

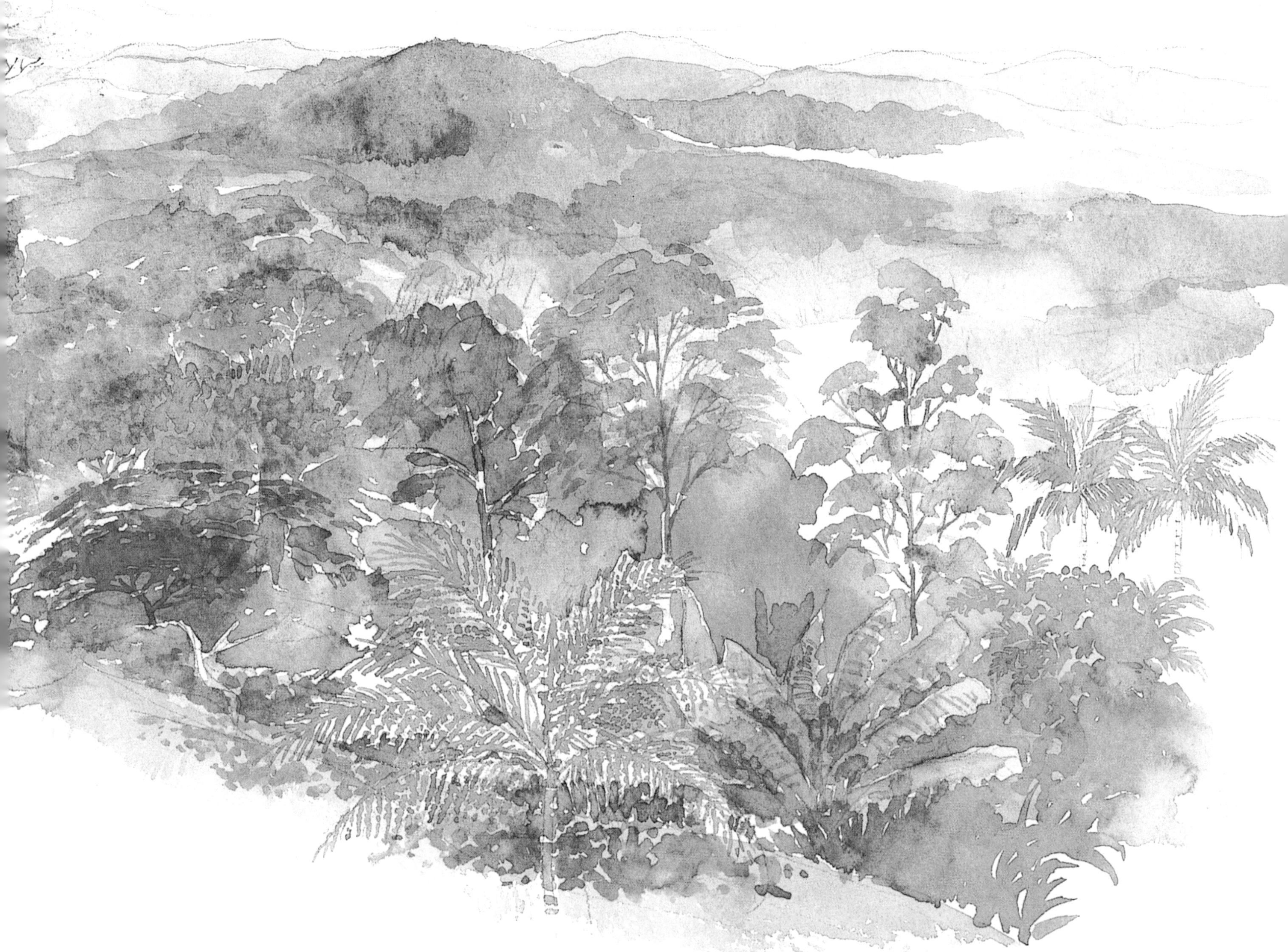

THE MAKING OF THAI SILK

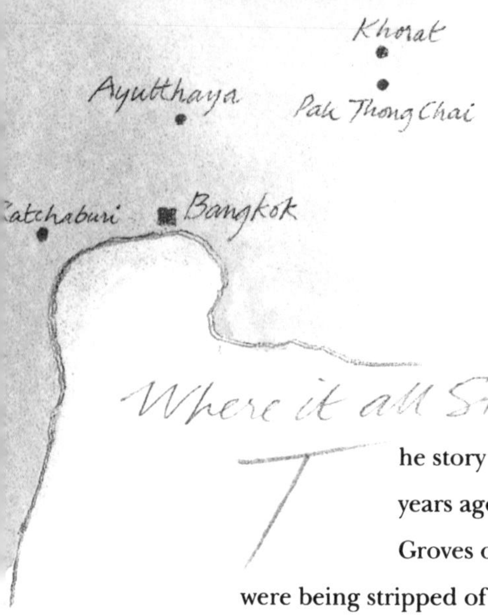

Where it all Started

The story of silk began more than four thousand years ago in the court of China's first emperor. Groves of mulberry trees in the palace gardens were being stripped of their leaves by tiny worms, which in turn had spun thousands of gossamer little cocoons. Noting this, a young concubine named Lei Tsu gathered some of the cocoons and, by way of experiment, dropped one in a basin of hot water. To her amazement, it began to unwind, forming an extraordinarily long thread of great strength yet as delicate as a spider's web. She was so delighted she did the same with others, using the thread to weave a splendid ceremonial robe for the emperor.

Such at least is the legendary origin of what one writer has described as "the finest natural textile thread known to man." There are other theories, as we shall see, but certainly China is where the art of weaving silk achieved widespread fame. Restricted at first to members of the imperial court, silk eventually spread to lower levels of Chinese society. Han rulers gave lengths of the precious fabric as diplomatic gifts and also used it to bribe the fierce nomadic tribesmen who occasionally threatened them. Gradually, a trade route to the West emerged, a tortuous passage known as the Silk Road which wandered through hostile lands and ended thousands of miles away at market places in the Middle East.

Not everyone approved of the supple, shimmering textile. "I see silken clothes, if you can call them clothes at all," wrote Seneca of Rome, "that in no degree afford protection either to the body or to the modesty of the wearer, and clad in which no woman could honestly say she is not naked." Such scoldings had little effect. Three centuries later another writer observed that "the use of silk which was once confined to the nobility is now spread to all classes without distinction, even to the lowest."

For centuries, however, only the Chinese knew the secrets of silk production. Exportation of silkworm eggs and mulberry cuttings was strictly prohibited, travelers were searched at the frontiers, and would-be smugglers were put to death. Inevitably, these efforts failed. Around 140 BC, both eggs and cuttings reached Khotan, in present-day Afghanistan, allegedly smuggled by a Chinese princess who went to marry the king and found the prospect of a silkless life unbearable.
From then it went to India, and a century later to Korea and Japan; around the same time the art was moving south with Chinese minority groups into present-day Indo-China and Thailand.

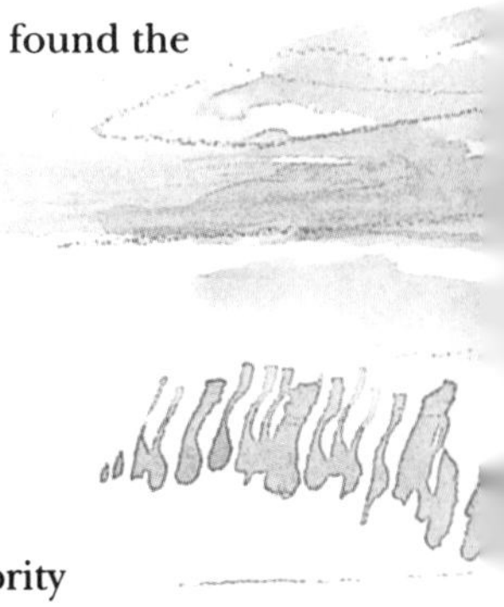

An alternative view holds that the art might have developed elsewhere independently, without the celebrity that accompanied its rise in China. A possible place is the Khorat

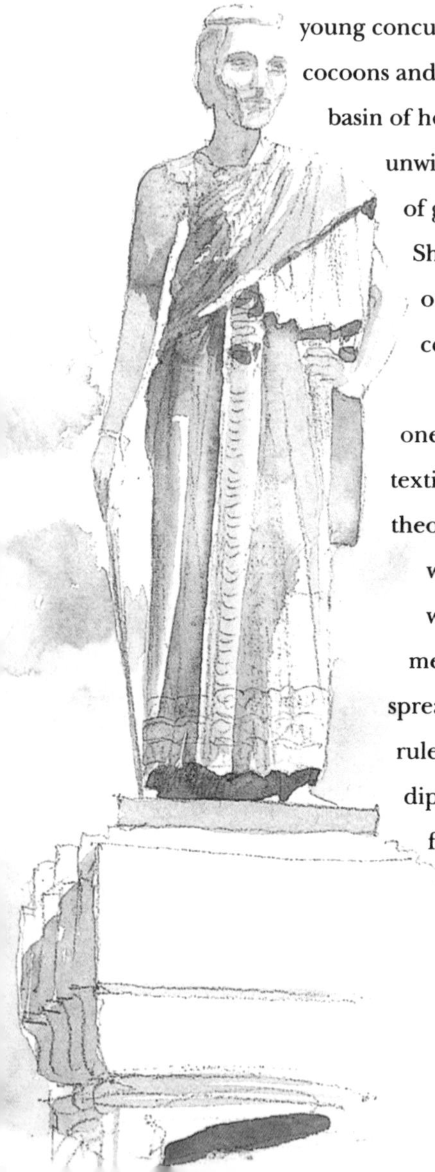

Thao Suranaree, the heroine of Khorat, who helped save the city from invaders in 1825. Khorat and other parts of the Northeast have long been centers of silk weaving.

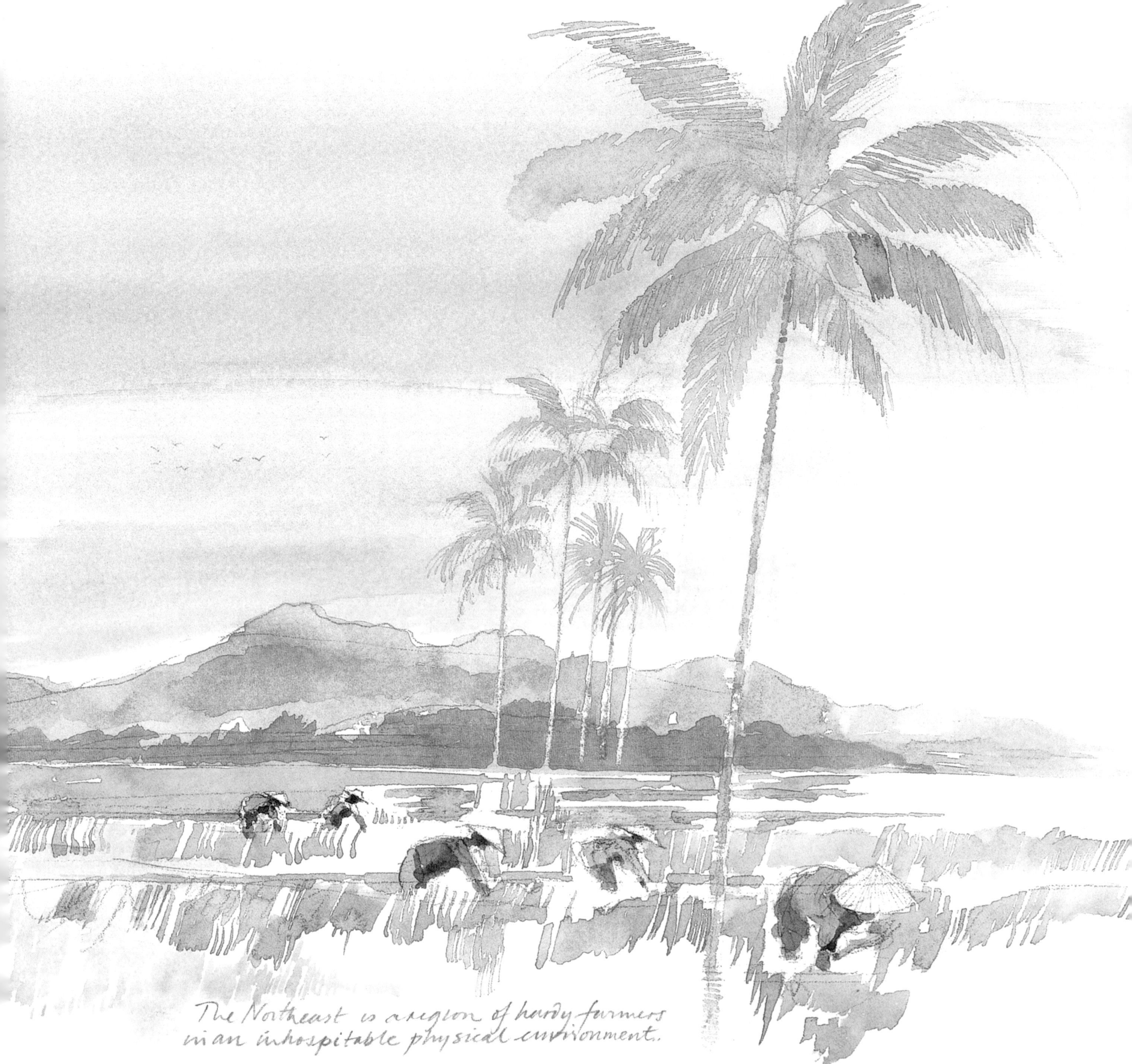

The Northeast is a region of hardy farmers in an inhospitable physical environment.

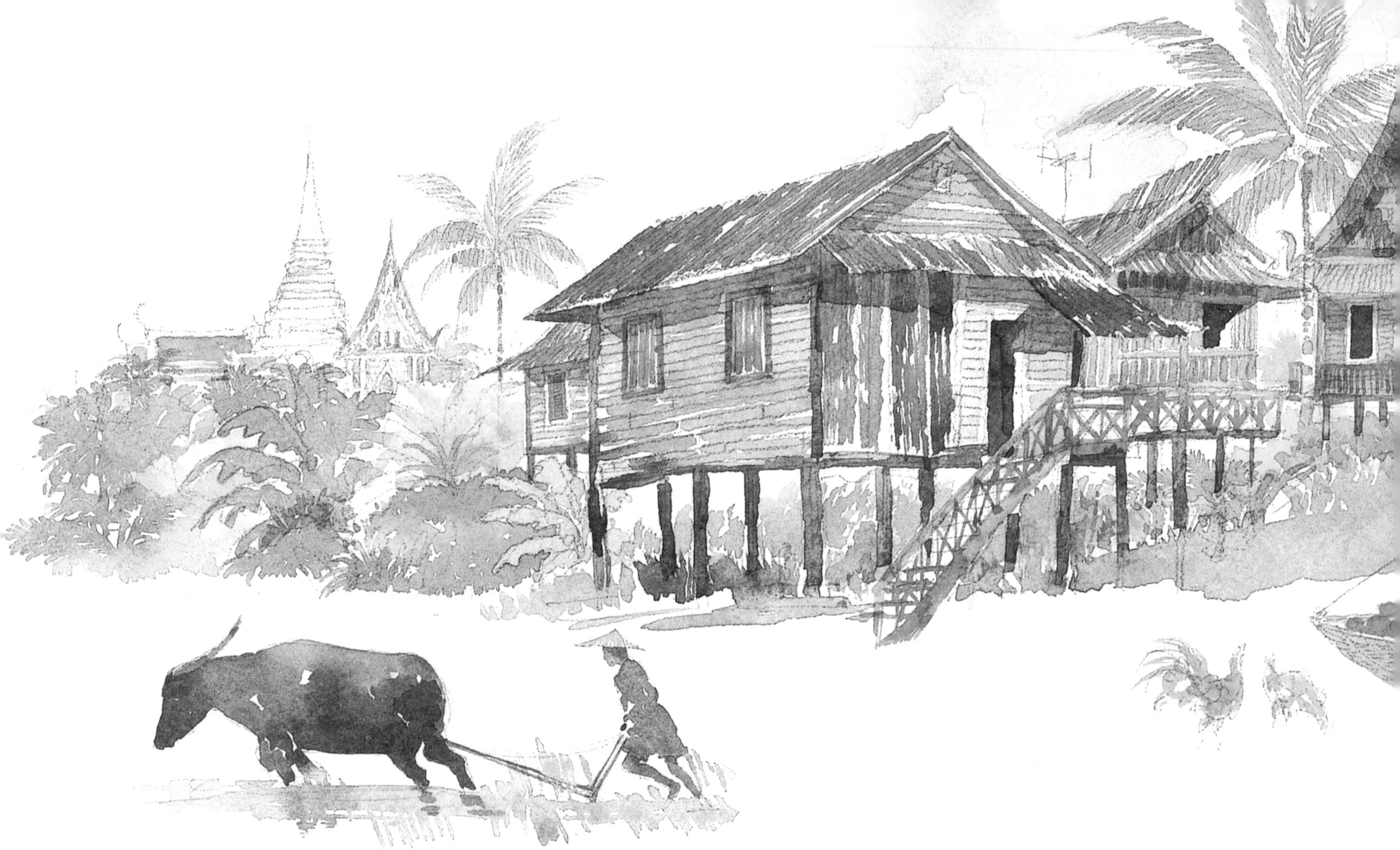

Plateau in northeastern Thailand, where some five thousand years ago a remarkable prehistoric culture known as Ban Chiang developed, numbering among its achievements rice cultivation and bronze metallurgy. During the 1960s, numerous excavations were made, both official and otherwise; and in one, about halfway down to the level of the earliest human habitation, a cluster of thread was found. Microscopic tests showed it to be silk, unwoven and undyed, while tests on surrounding artifacts indicated they were between four and five thousand years old.

Pending further discovery, it would be rash to claim the rather mysterious people of Ban Chiang cultivated silk long before the Thais arrived. What is undeniable, however, is the fact that silk weaving has long been a specialty of the Northeast and still flourishes in countless villages.

Jim Thompson saw the looms when he first visited the region, shortly after his arrival in Thailand. It was then regarded as remote. Magnificent ruins survived from the time it had been a part of the Khmer empire, and residents of Khorat honored a

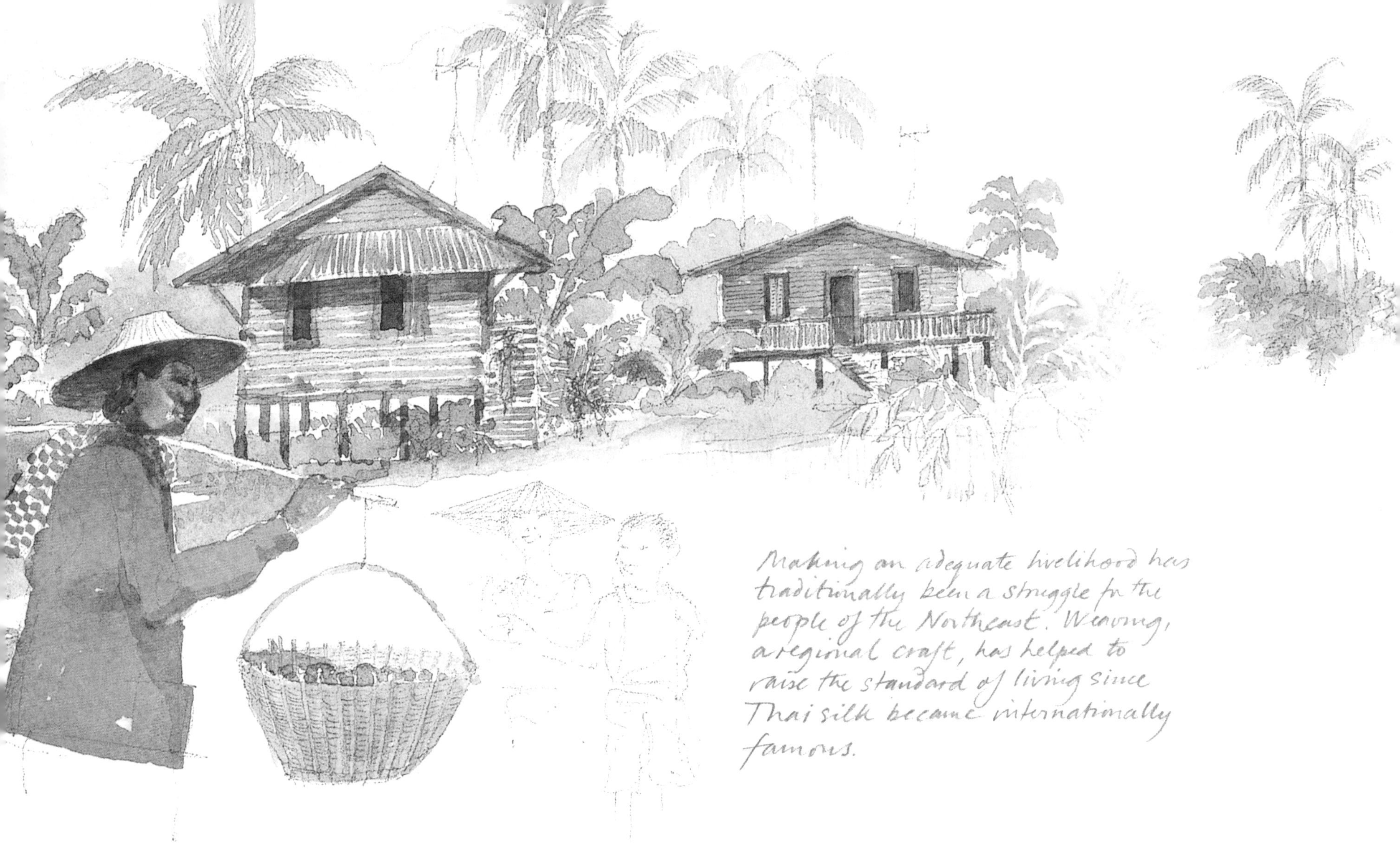

Making an adequate livelihood has traditionally been a struggle for the people of the Northeast. Weaving, a regional craft, has helped to raise the standard of living since Thai silk became internationally famous.

local heroine named Thao Suranaree (Khunying Mo), who had saved the town from Laotian invaders in 1826; but there were few paved roads, and life was hard for most residents.

Yet silk was an integral part of life in the Northeast, and many of the pieces produced on its simple looms were of high quality, displaying intricate patterns and weaving techniques. Working in her spare time, whenever free from the more important tasks of planting and harvesting crops, a girl was expected to weave at least two superior pieces, one for her wedding outfit and other to present to her future husband.

A number of the lengths Jim Thompson took to America in his first collection came from the Northeast, and most of the silk used for costumes in *The King and I* came from a small village called Pak Thong Chai near Khorat. Today silk weaving remains the region's predominant handicraft — more so than ever, indeed, since the product now attracts admirers far from the mulberry groves and the carefully tended little worms who still perform the miracle that so amazed the legendary Lei Tsu.

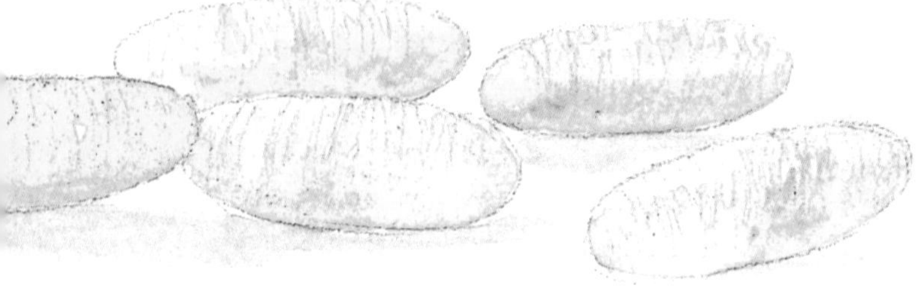

These golden-yellow cocoons are but one of the several stages of sericulture, which begins with hatching the silkworm eggs and finally ends with the unreeling of the miraculous fiber.

The Traditional Way of Making Silk

Despite revolutionary changes in methods of manufacture, the ultimate basis of silk remains a tiny, inconspicuous-looking worm with a voracious appetite for mulberry leaves. Nothing would be possible without the efforts of this little creature, and the most critical period in silk production comes during its brief life span of around 20 days.

Nearly all silkworm-producing moths belong to the family Bombycidae, of which one member, *Bombyx mori* is responsible for most of the world's silk. Believed to be native to China, it no longer exists in the wild; after so many centuries of inbreeding, it is incapable of flight, mates quickly after emerging from its chrysalis, and dies a day or so after laying its eggs.

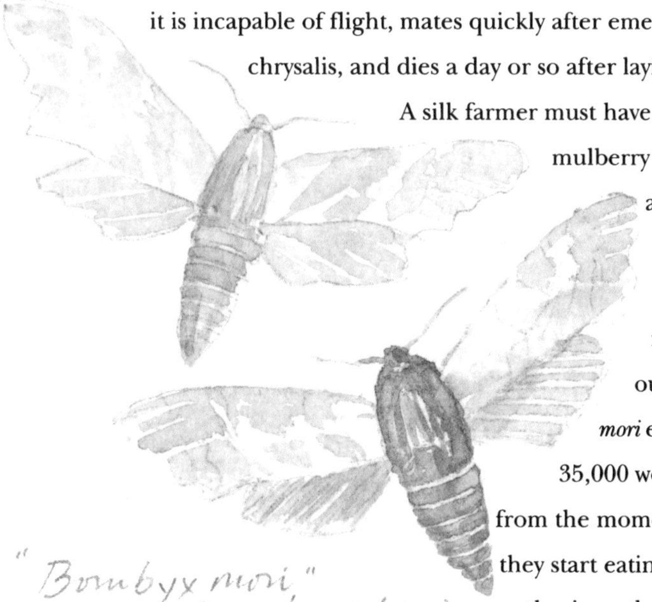

A silk farmer must have a ready supply of mulberry close at hand, and once the trees produce new leaves he begins rearing. An ounce of *Bombyx mori* eggs yields about 35,000 worms, and almost from the moment they emerge they start eating with an enthusiasm that never abates.

"Bombyx mori," which no longer exists in the wild, is the moth responsible for most of the silk produced in the world today.

Members of the farmer's household must spend a growing amount of time tending to their bamboo trays of hungry worms, whose constant chewing has been likened to "the falling of light rain on leaves."

After about three weeks the worms suddenly stop eating and raise their heads: a sign that they are ready for the all-important job of spinning cocoons. At this stage, they are moved from their trays to bamboo scaffolding, which will make the cocoons more uniform in shape and easier to collect.

Each silkworm now doubles itself up on its back, and by contracting secretes a steady stream of liquid silk, coated with sericin, which hardens on exposure to air. After some 36 hours, the worm is sealed within a yellow cocoon, embarked on the process of metamorphosing into a moth.

Reeling is another labor-intensive task which must be done within ten days before the moths begin to break through their silk wrapping. The cocoons are immersed in hot water to kill the chrysalis, after which the silk thread — anywhere from 200 to 1,000 yards (180 to 910 meters) per cocoon — is hand-reeled into a uniform strand of raw silk. This is then spun into even skeins and soaked in hot water to remove the sericin coating.

Local silk is used for the *wefts*, the threads that pass across the looms; while the *warps*, those stretched lengthwise, are imported. The warps are fine, even, and strong, having been "thrown" or twisted to increase the tensile strength and elasticity. The Thai wefts, on the other hand, are coarse, uneven, and fluffy.

Worms hatched from "Bombyx mori" eggs live exclusively on a diet of mulberry leaves, eating increasing quantities as they mature.

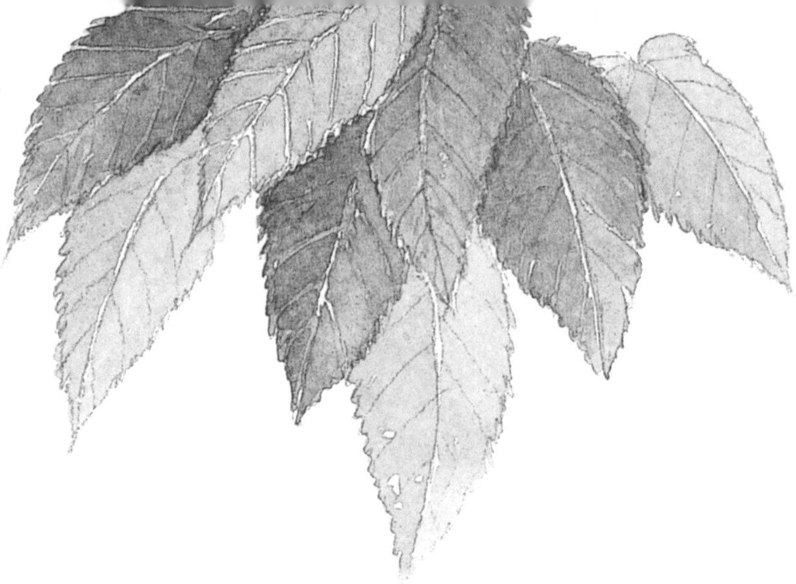

Together, the two give the silk its distinctive luster and texture, impossible to achieve in cloth woven on a power-loom with only one kind of yarn.

After being dyed, the warp silk is dried in the sun and then unwound by a hand spinning wheel to form a yarn package of suitable size. A number of these are placed on a bamboo creel and the yarn from all is drawn on a warping board; made into chains, it is set aside until the time comes for setting up the looms.

For a length of silk 40 inches (1 meter) wide, over a thousand strands of warp silk are set by hand on either a traditional throwing shuttle loom or a Chinese flying shuttle. In Thailand, the latter is generally used in weaving plain silk, while the first is more suitable for fancier weaves like brocades — a single piece of which may take as long as three months to produce.

A view of the Jim Thompson farm from a neighboring hill, showing the farm buildings, the research center and the filature plant, together with its vast acreage of mulberry bushes.

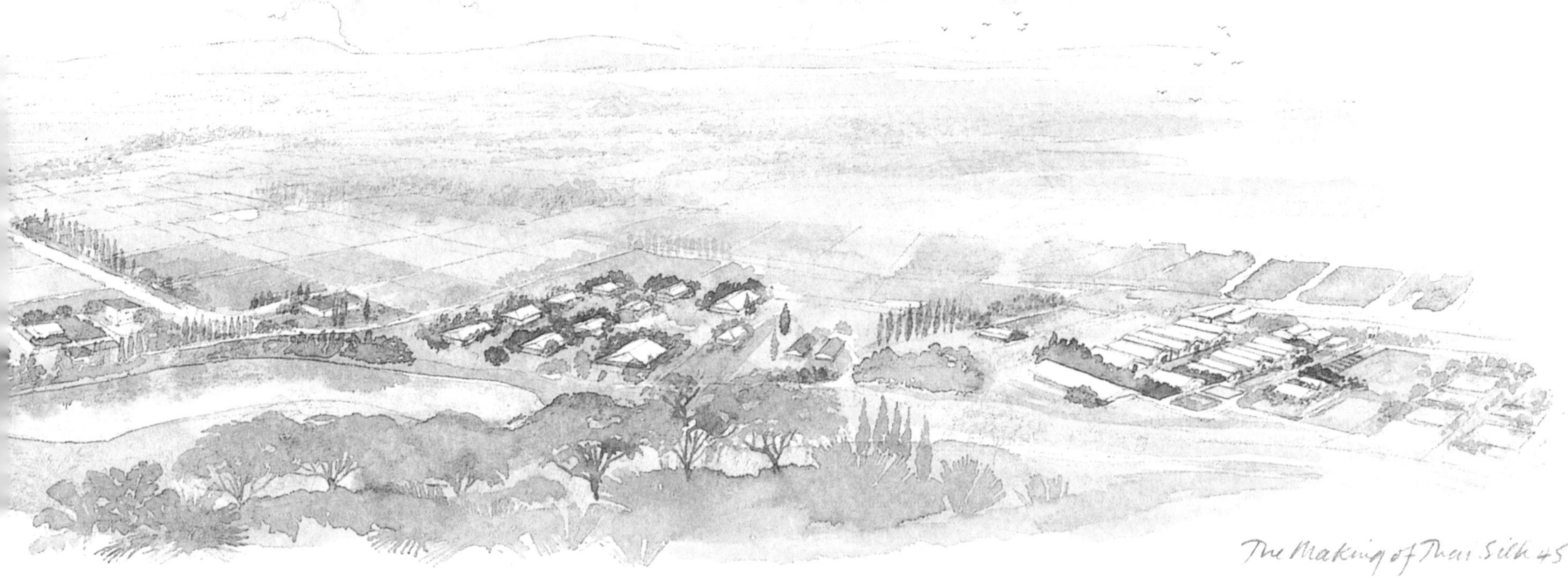

The Farms and the Factory

Pak Thong Chai, a peaceful village not far from the northeastern city of Nakhon Ratchasima (Khorat), has long figured significantly in the story of the company founded by Jim Thompson. It was here, on travels through the region in the late 1940s, that he discovered some of his earliest weavers, producing beautiful silks on simple looms in the open spaces under their raised wooden houses.

At that time, all the silk that Jim Thompson sold was produced by weavers working independently, an arrangement that suited both Jim Thompson's temperament and the prevailing conditions. As silk became a major industry, however, requiring ever greater quantities and stricter quality control, the company decided to bring most of its operations, from silkworm rearing to weaving and printing, under its own supervision. Suitably, in view of its proximity to the traditional centers of Thai silk production, the place selected for the project was Pak Thong Chai.

Here, too, mulberry farms have been established, covering more than 1,000 acres (400 hectares), together with facilities for raising the all-important silkworms and harvesting their cocoons. About ten miles (16 kilometers) away is the factory, the largest of its kind in the world, where the silk is woven and printed.

Thus in an area that reflects the very essence of rural Thailand, the Jim Thompson company has moved silk weaving into the modern world without destroying the unique qualities that brought it renown half a century ago.

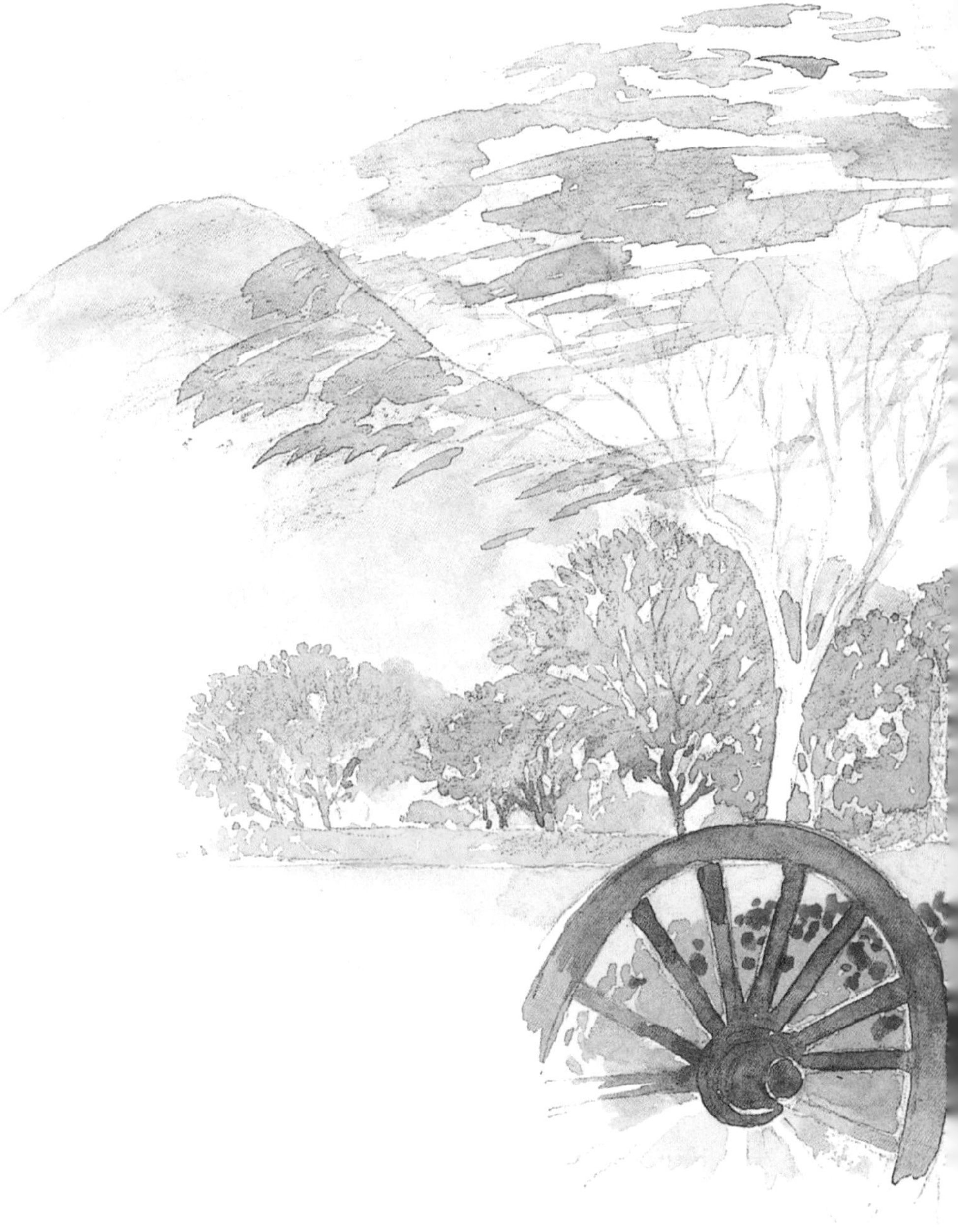

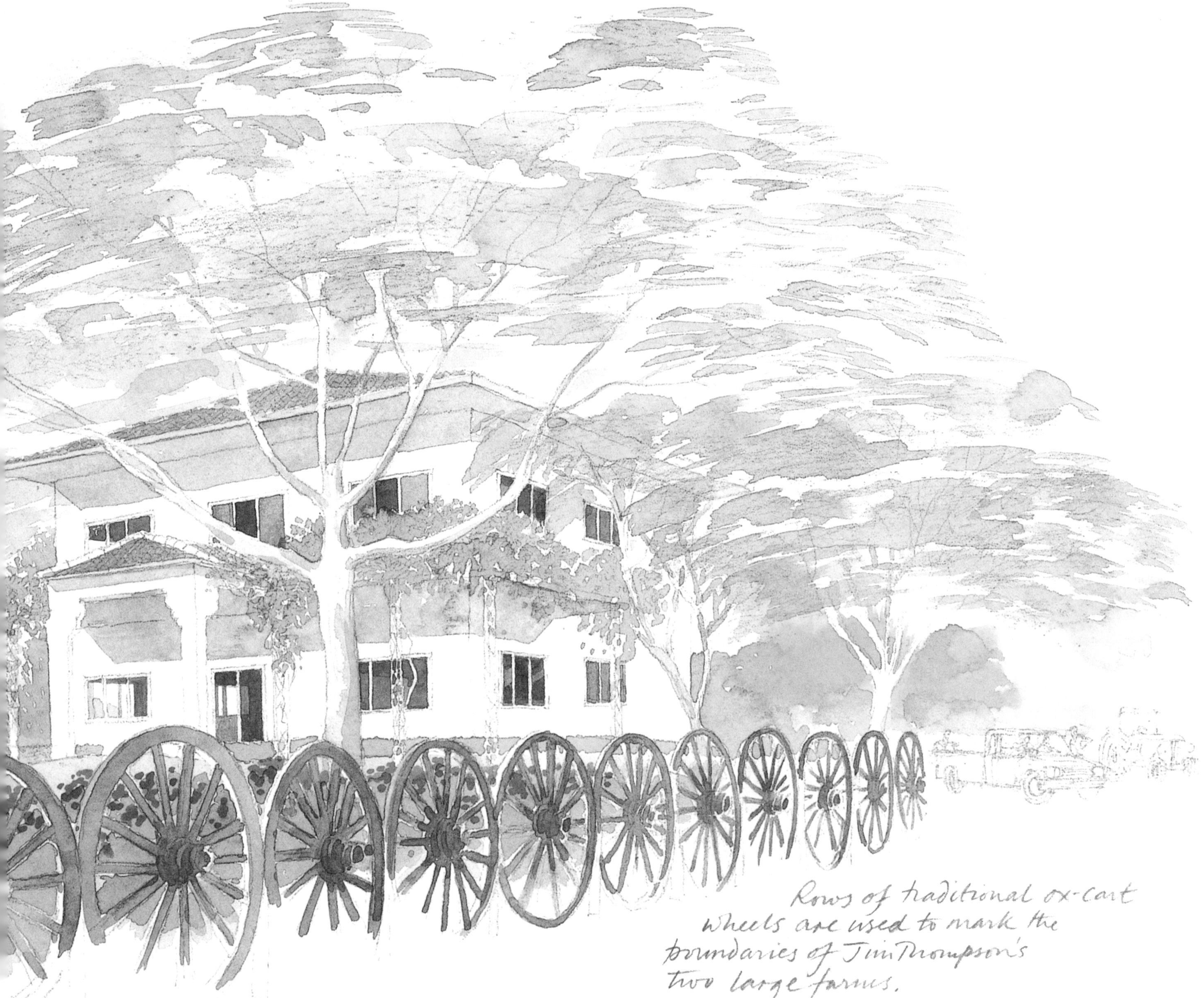

Rows of traditional ox-cart wheels are used to mark the boundaries of Jim Thompson's two large farms.

Mulberry pickers spend much of their time picking leaves for hungry worms. The worms feed almost continuously until they are ready to spin their cocoons.

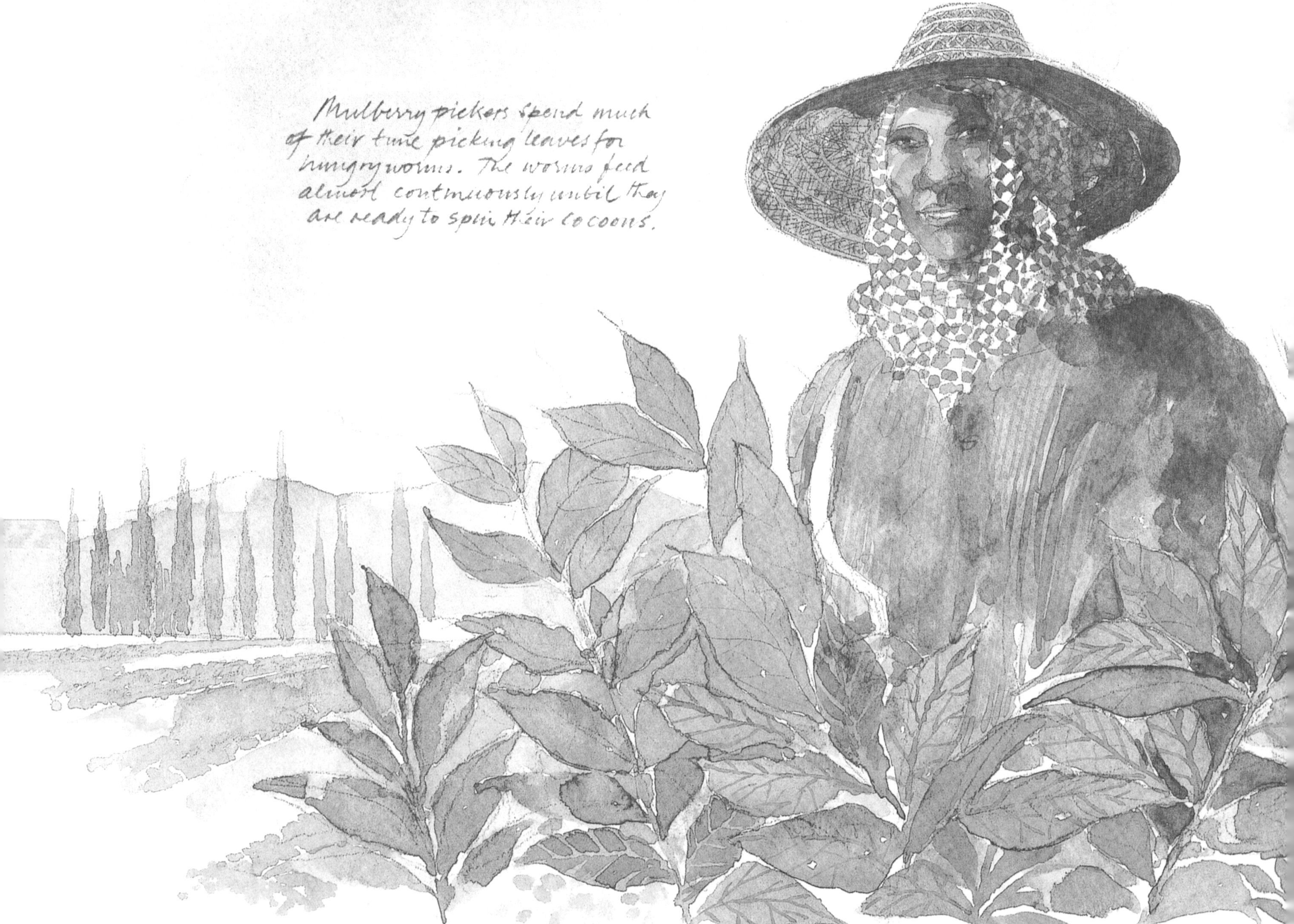

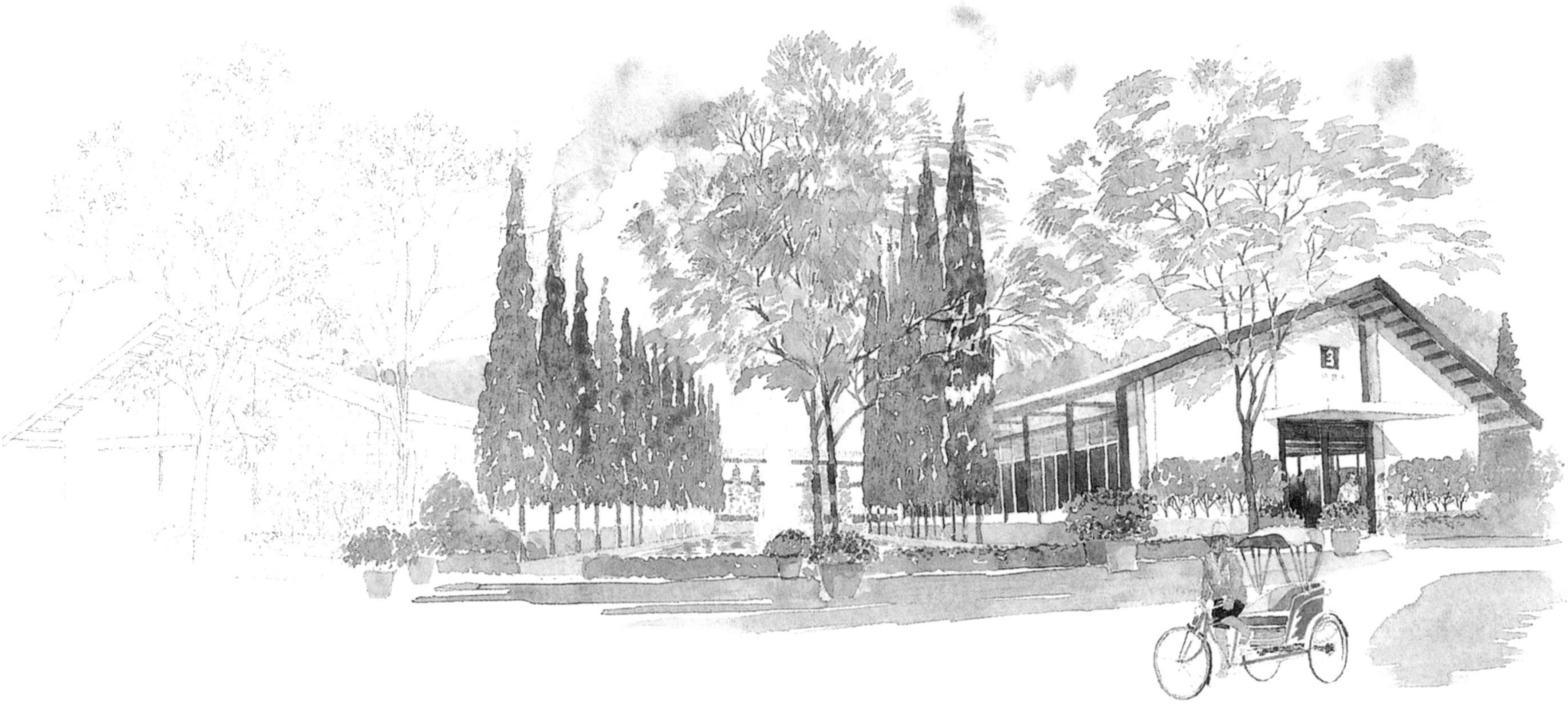

The Jim Thompson factory at Pak Thong Chai, the largest handweaving facility of its kind in the world, accommodates over 500 hand looms as well as many modern power looms.

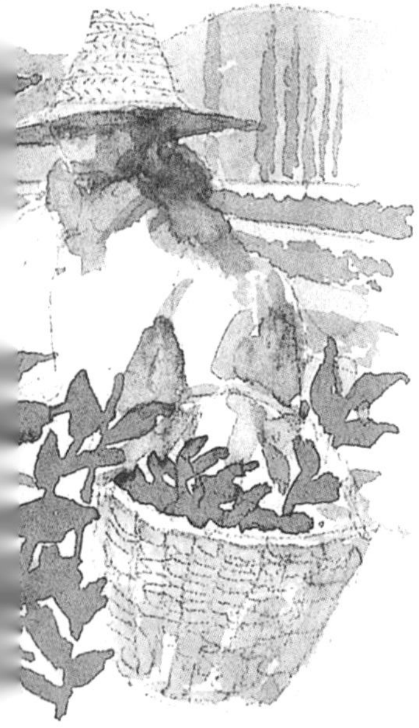

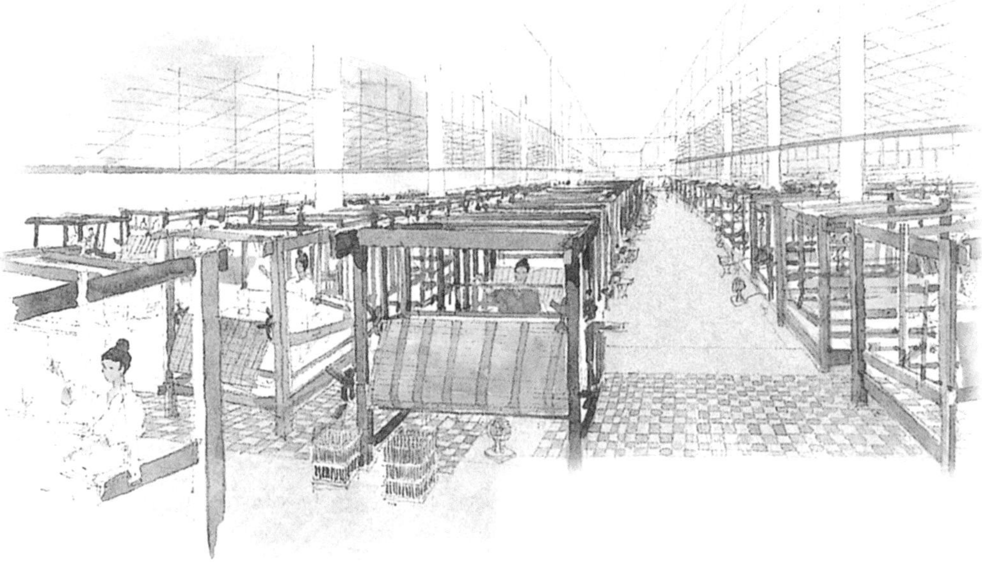

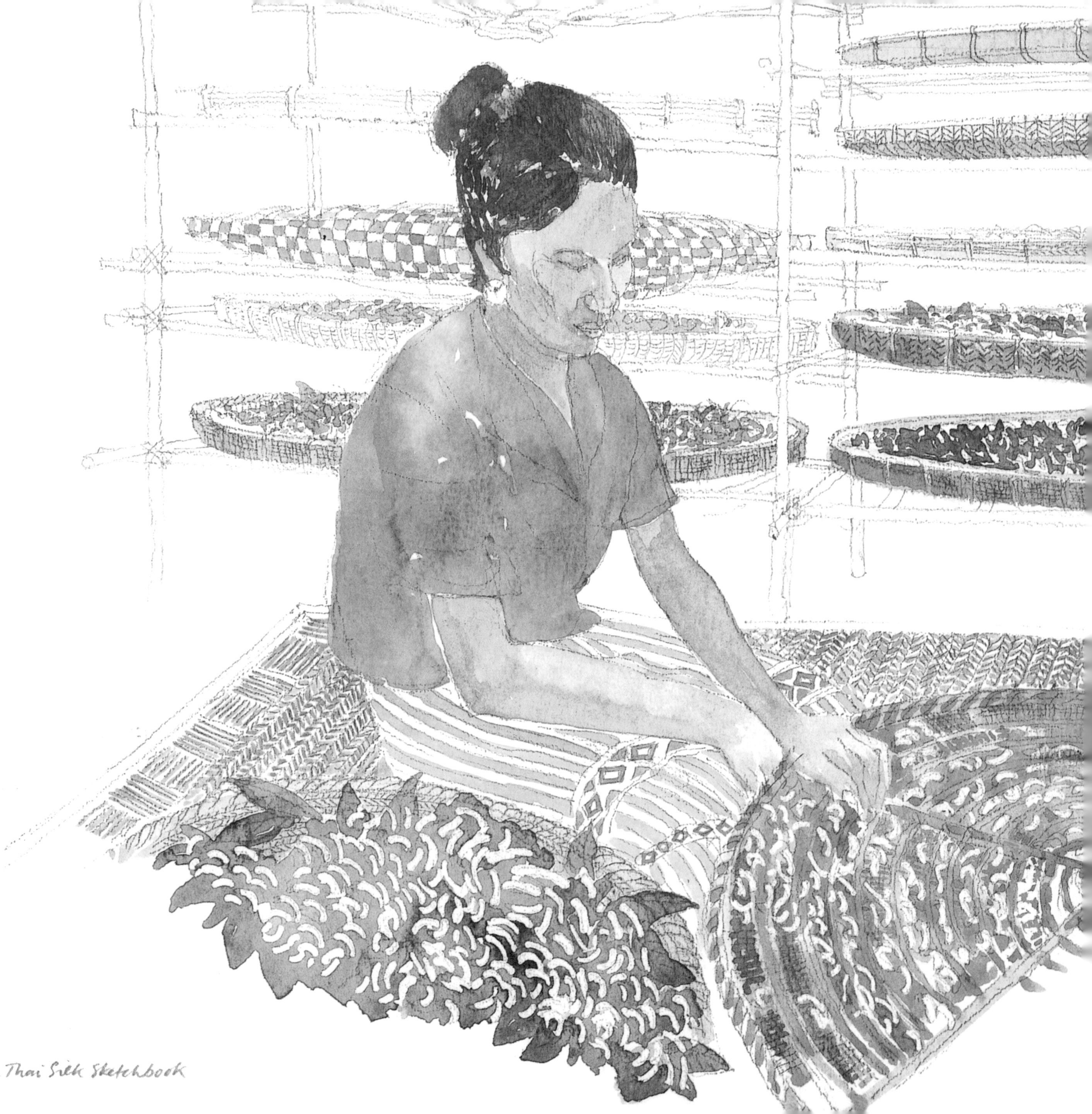

From Worm to Cocoon

The young, rapidly growing silkworms are kept on shelves in flat bamboo trays and supplied with fresh mulberry leaves several times a day. They are protected from harmful flying insects by wrapping the trays in homespun cotton.

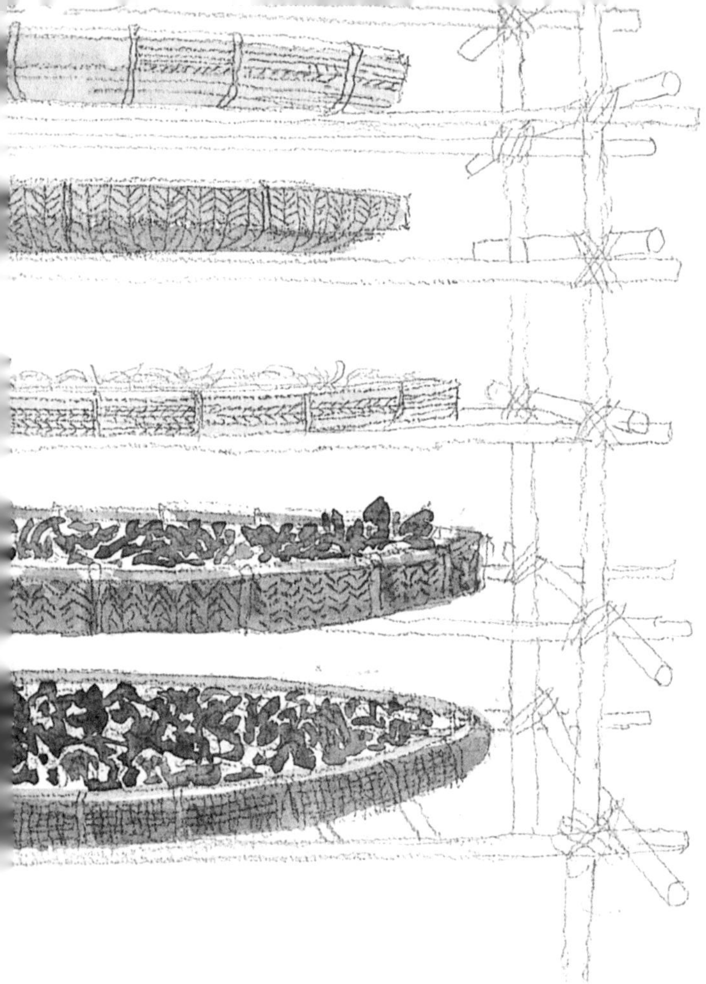

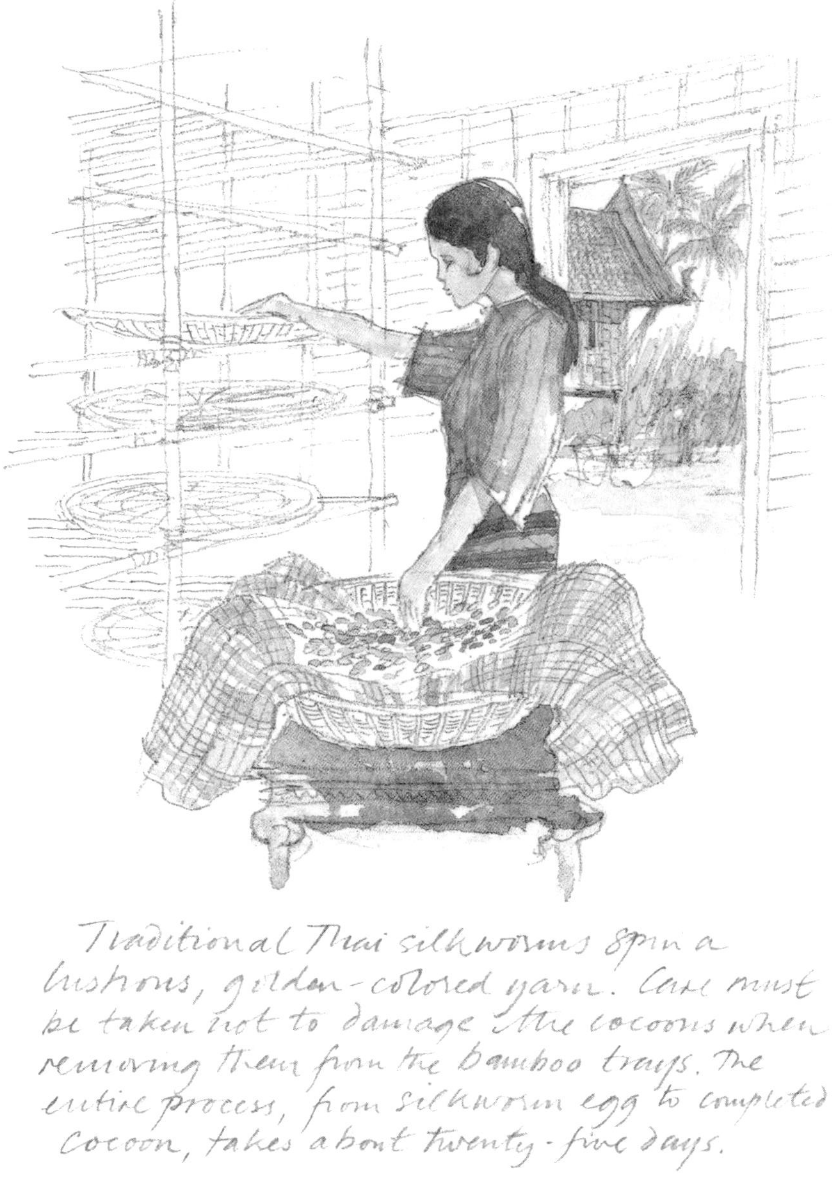

After feeding voraciously for about twenty-four days, the plump silkworms are ready to spin their cocoons and must be transferred gently to specially woven circular trays.

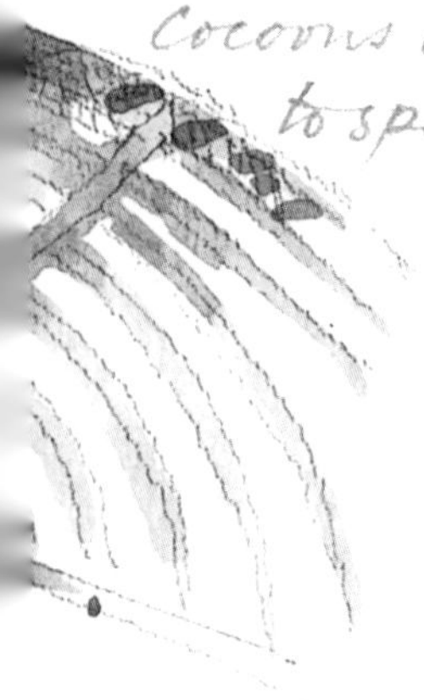

Traditional Thai silkworms spin a lustrous, golden-colored yarn. Care must be taken not to damage the cocoons when removing them from the bamboo trays. The entire process, from silkworm egg to completed cocoon, takes about twenty-five days.

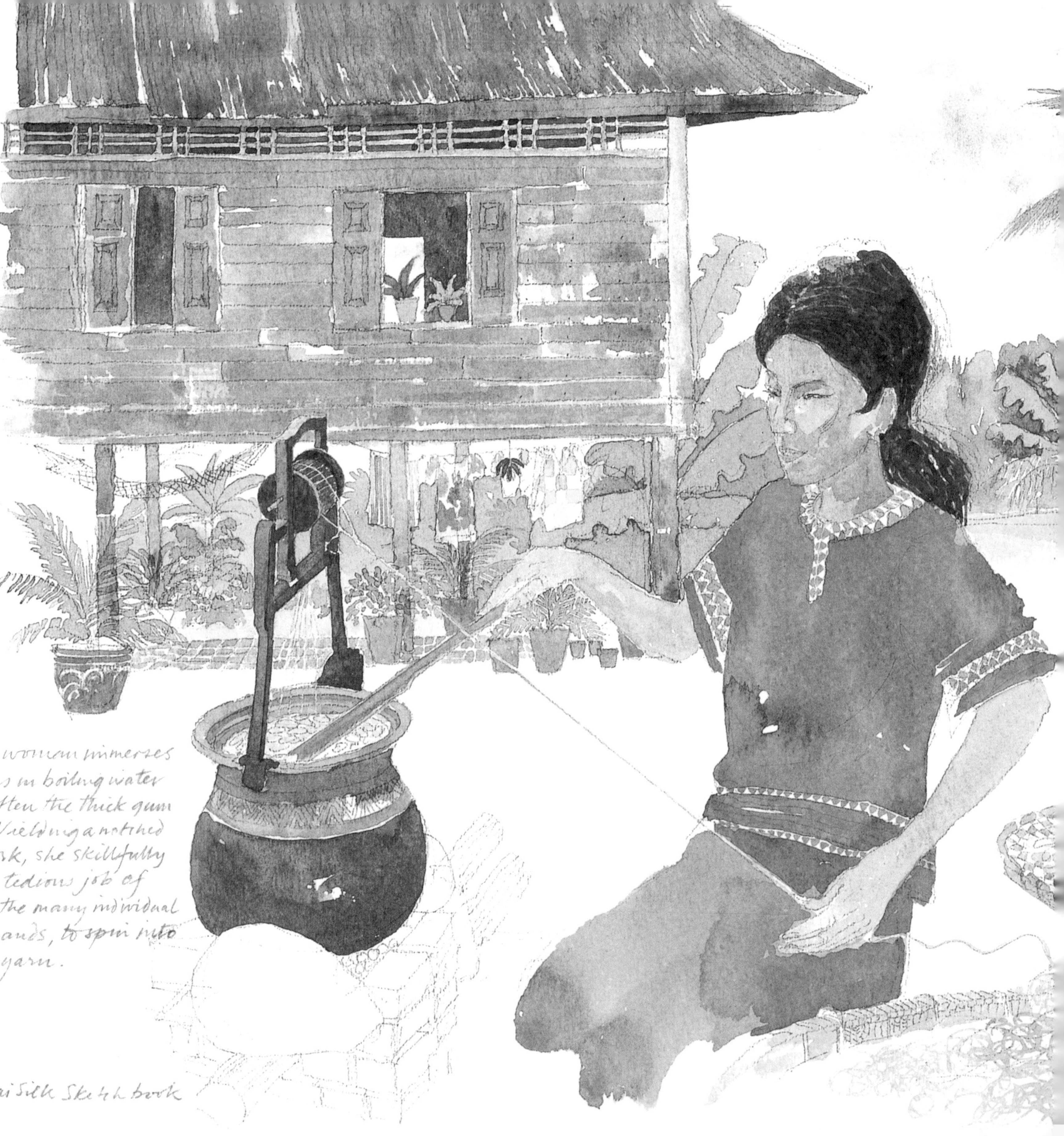

A village woman immerses the cocoons in boiling water to help soften the thick gum coating. Wielding a notched wooden fork, she skillfully begins the tedious job of unreeling the many individual cocoon strands, to spin into a single yarn.

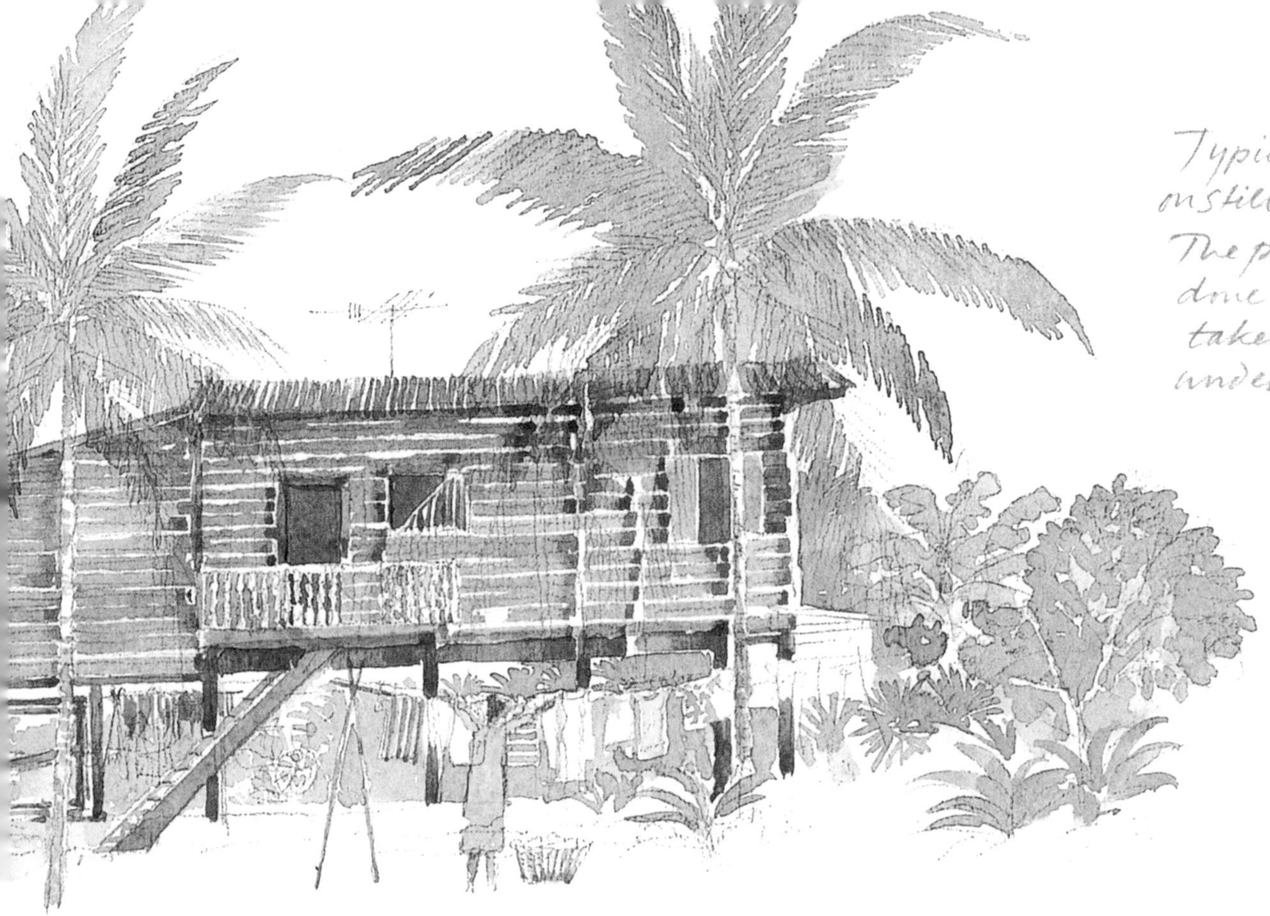

Typically, village houses are raised on stilts for maximum air circulation. The process of silk making, usually done by women of the community, takes place in the open area under the house.

In the village, fresh cocoons are reeled as soon as possible after spinning is completed. This tray of golden cocoons is ready to be scooped into the reeling pot as needed. A colorful piece of hand-woven silk helps to protect the fragile cocoons from damage.

Reeling the Silk

Each cocoon consists of many yards of tightly woven silken thread. In the reeling process, a special wooden device is used to locate the end of the filament, after which it must be carefully unwound, a process that not only requires hard work over a boiling pot but also practiced skill to keep the threads unbroken.

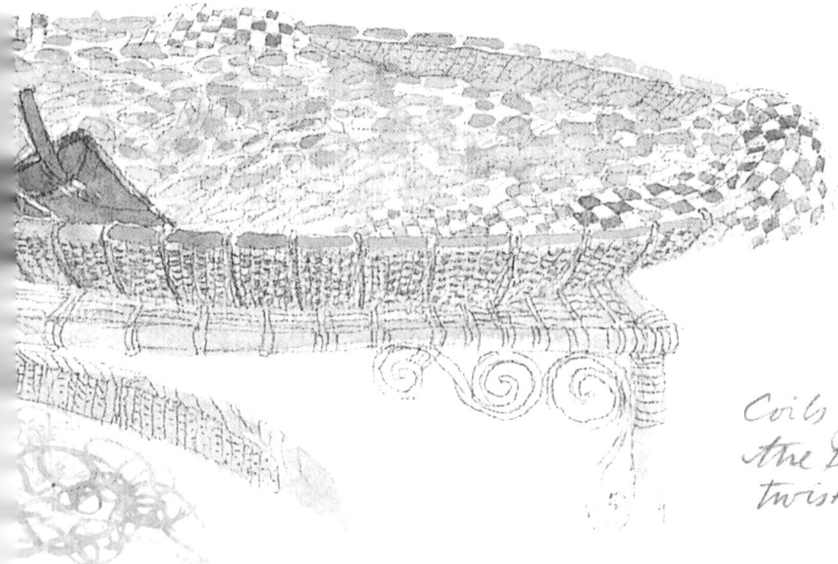

Coils of golden yarn pile up in the bamboo basket, ready to be twisted into skeins for safekeeping.

Preparing the Yarn and Dyeing

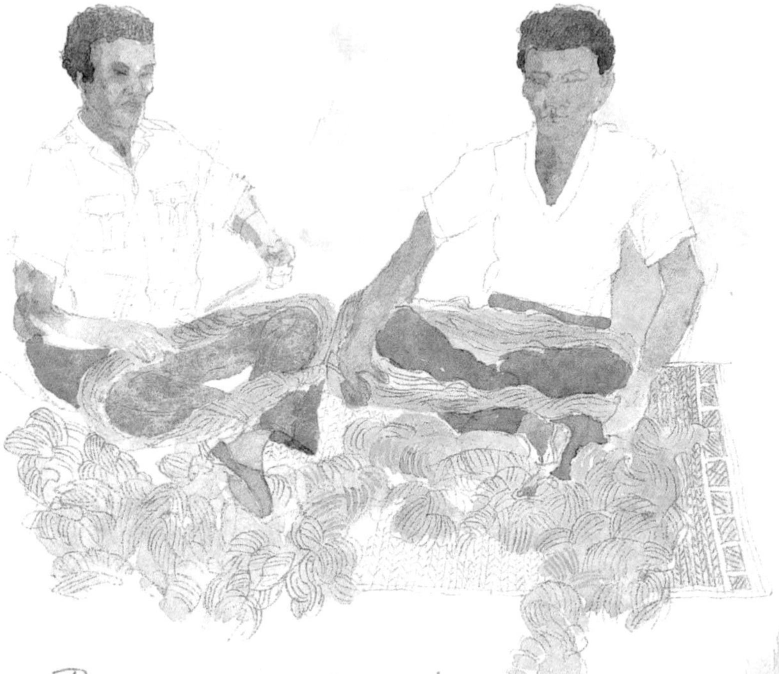

These men are preparing raw silk skeins prior to their being plunged into a boiling bath to remove the thick gum coating.

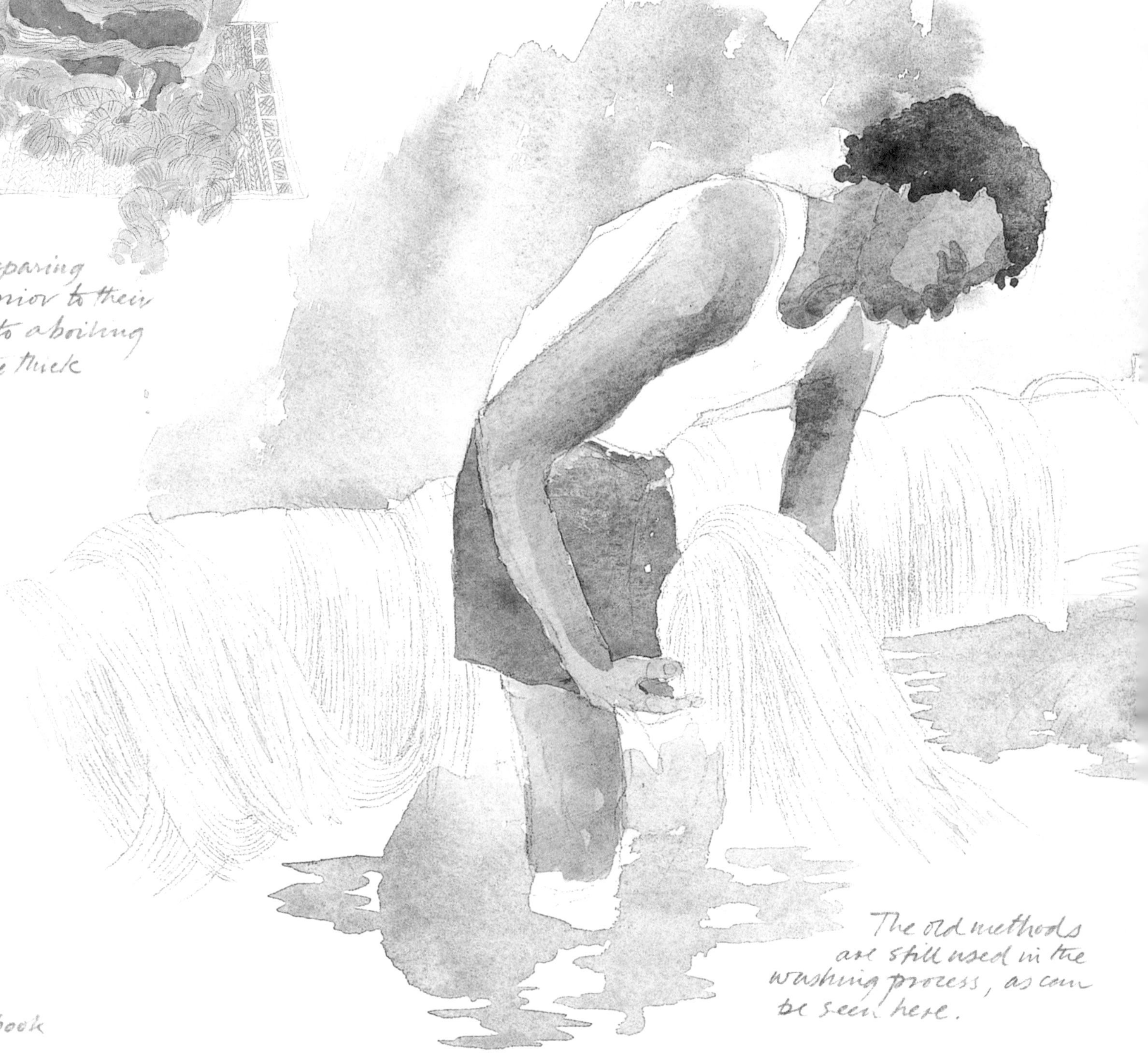

The old methods are still used in the washing process, as can be seen here.

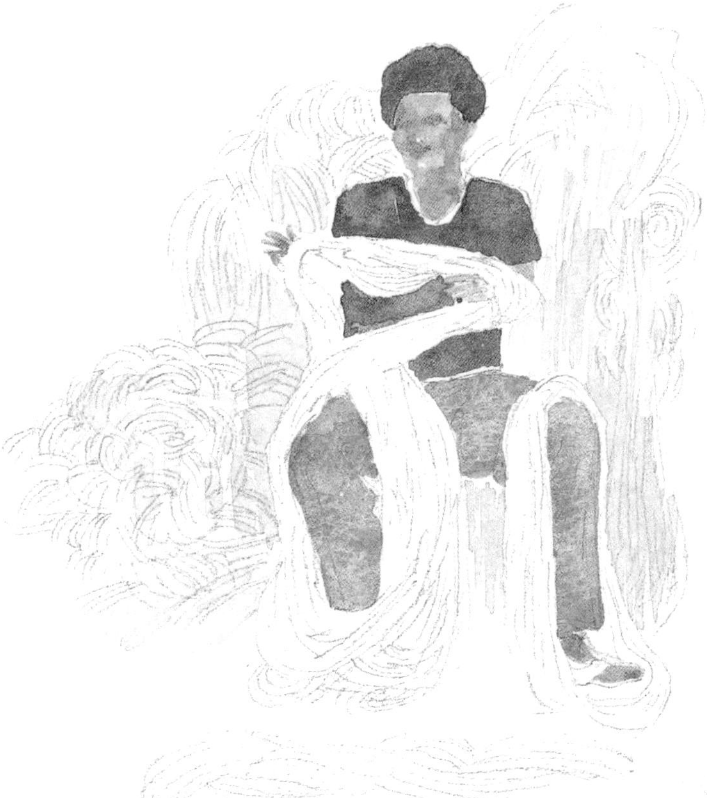

After a thorough washing and degumming, the skeins are prepared for dyeing.

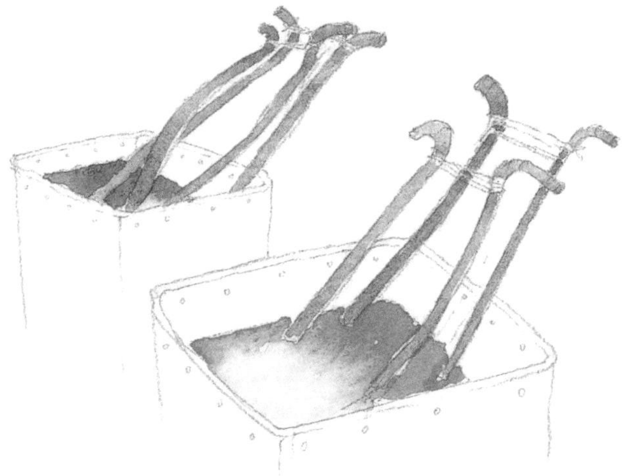

The skeins of degummed silk are placed on bamboo rods, then immersed in tins of hot water containing dyes of the desired colors

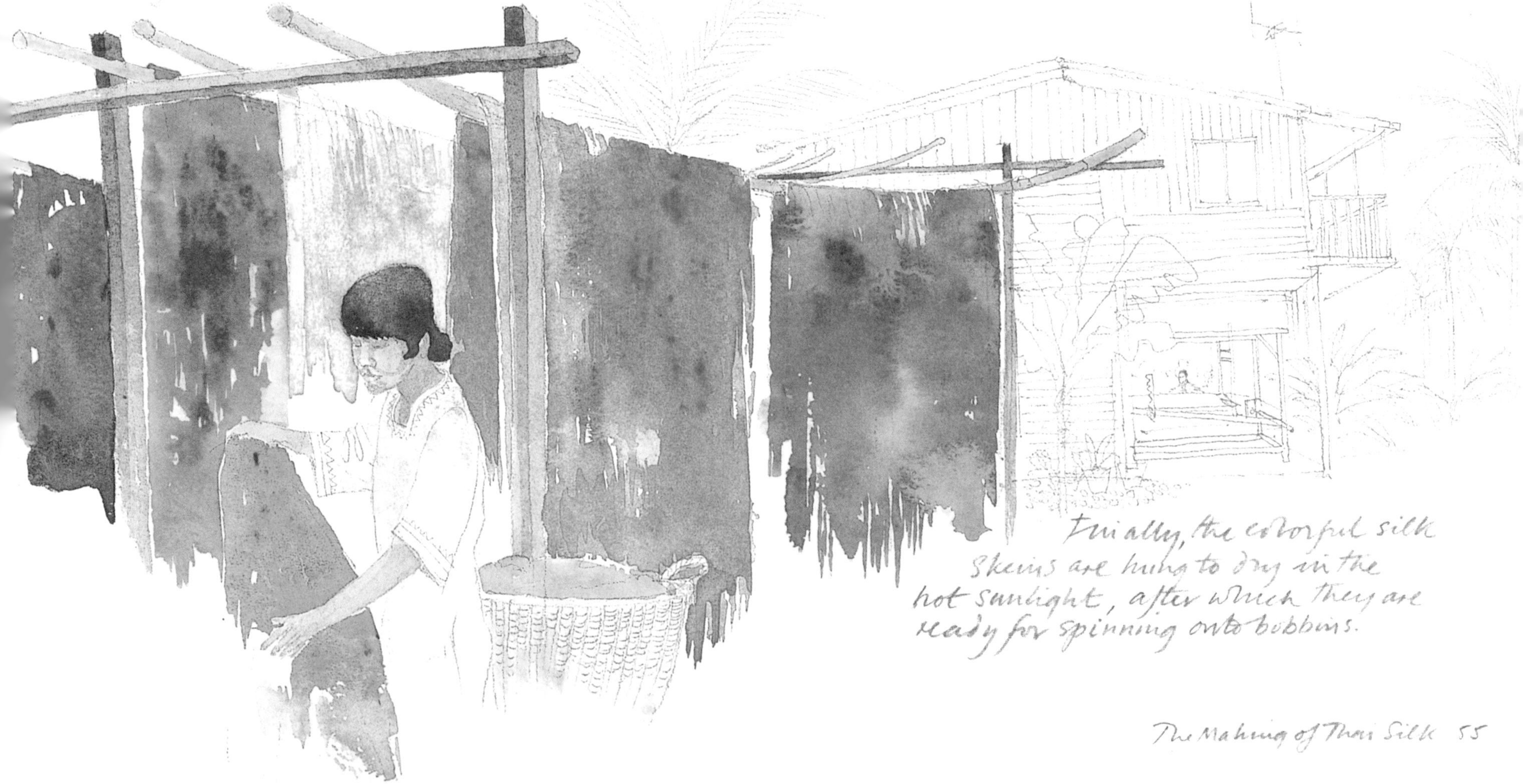

Finally, the colorful silk skeins are hung to dry in the hot sunlight, after which they are ready for spinning onto bobbins.

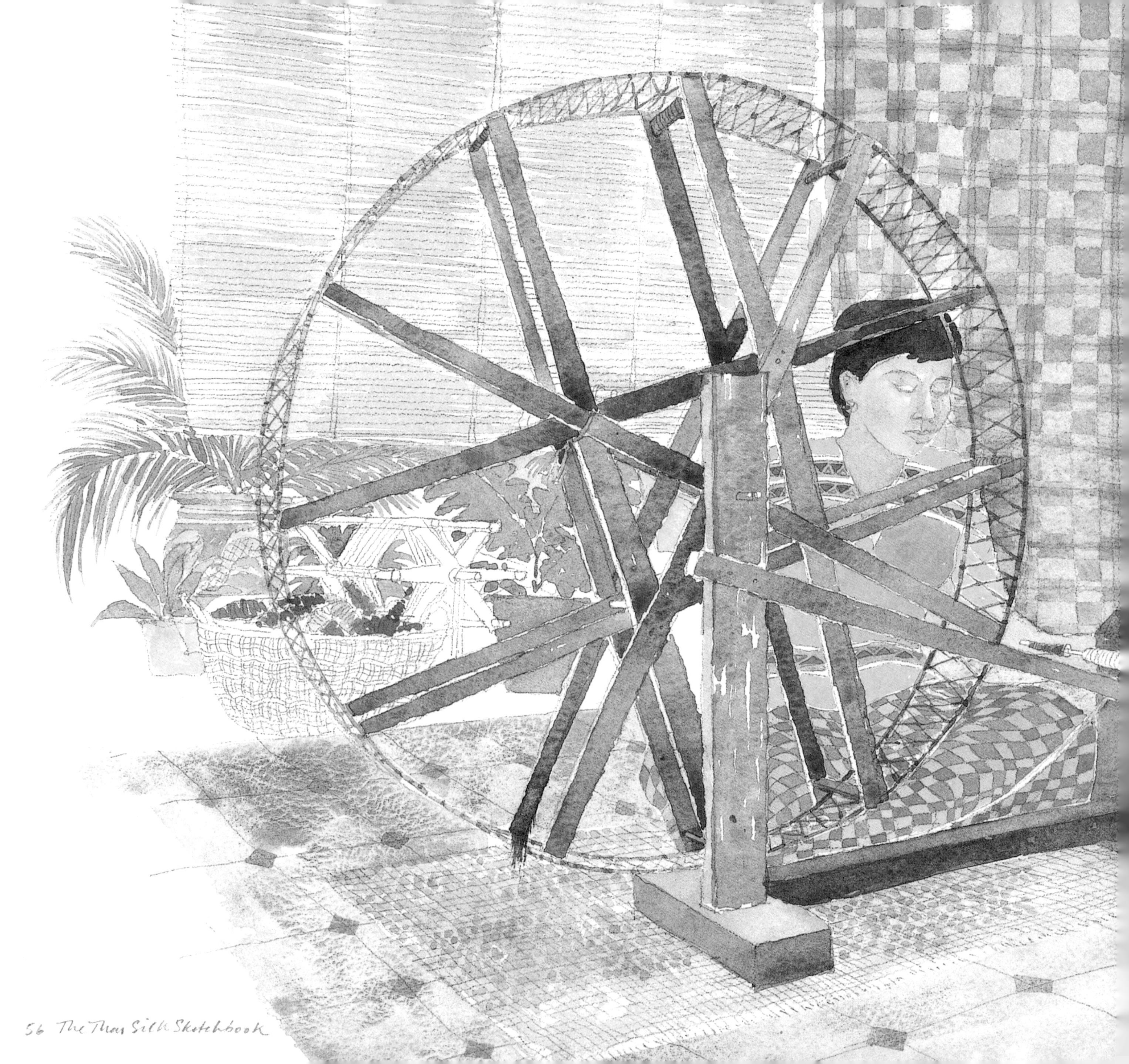

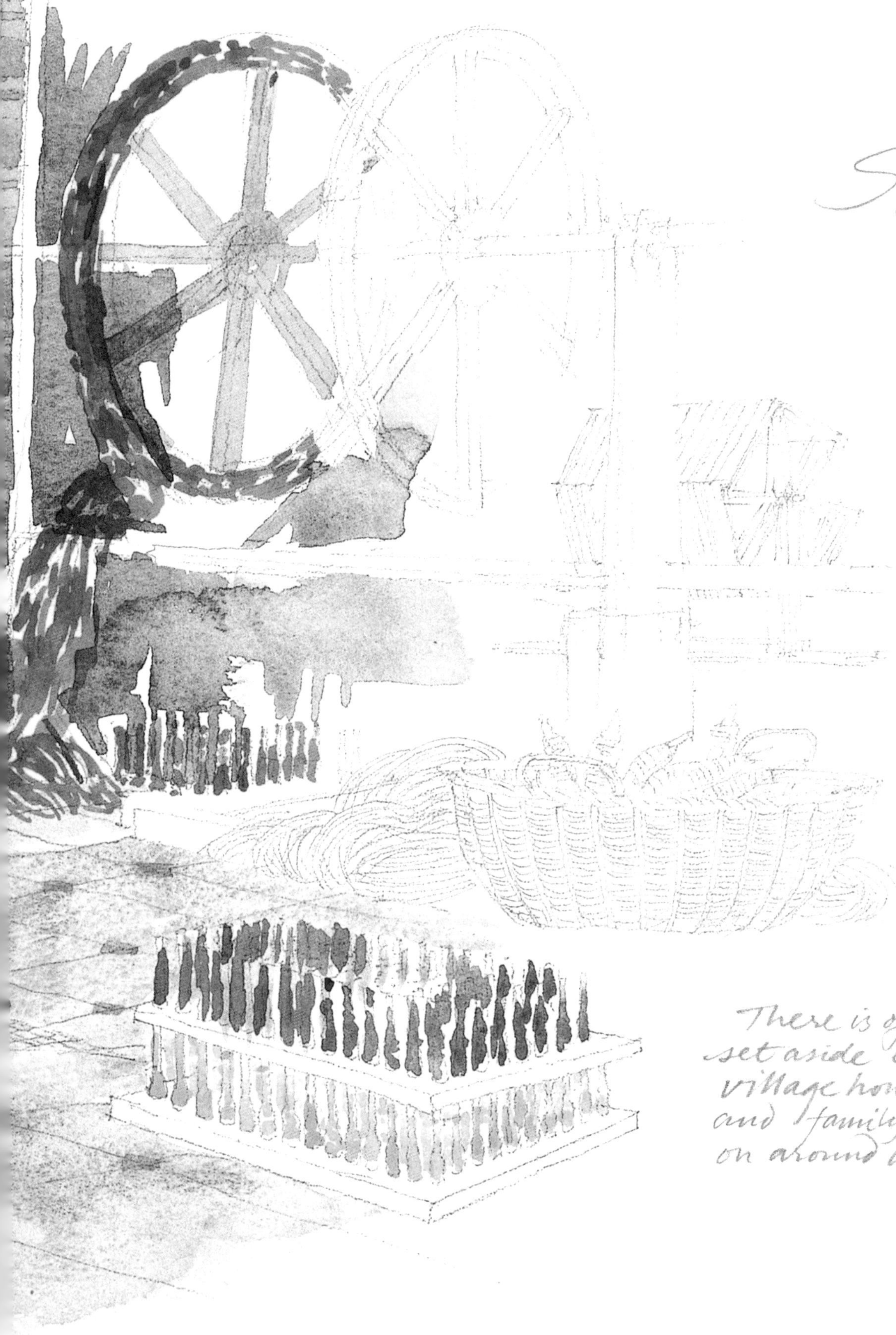

Spinning

Even today, despite the introduction of a wide range of new techniques, the traditional spinning wheel is still necessary for a variety of purposes.

Spinning wheels are used for unwinding dyed silk skeins onto big bobbins for the warping process, winding pirns or small bobbins for the weaving shuttle, and plying yarns together for weaving heavier-weight fabrics.

There is often a space set aside on the floor of village houses for spinning and family life carries on around it.

Setting up the Warp

The lengthwise threads of a woven material are called the warp, made by pulling yarns from bobbins onto the warping frame. The average warp has over 2,400 individual ends and – however careful the warper may be – it is impossible to prevent some threads from breaking. Such threads must be carefully watched and immediately mended.

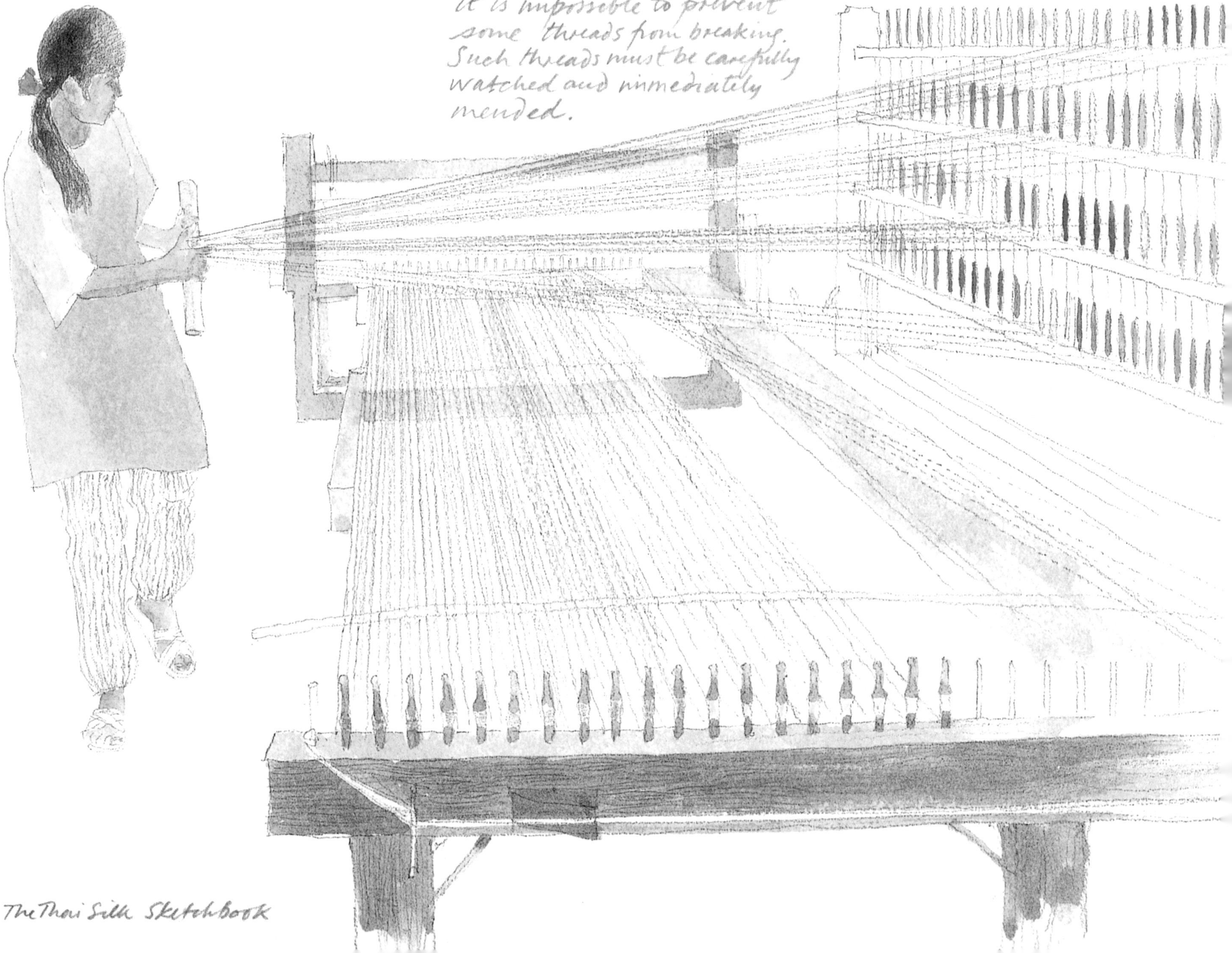

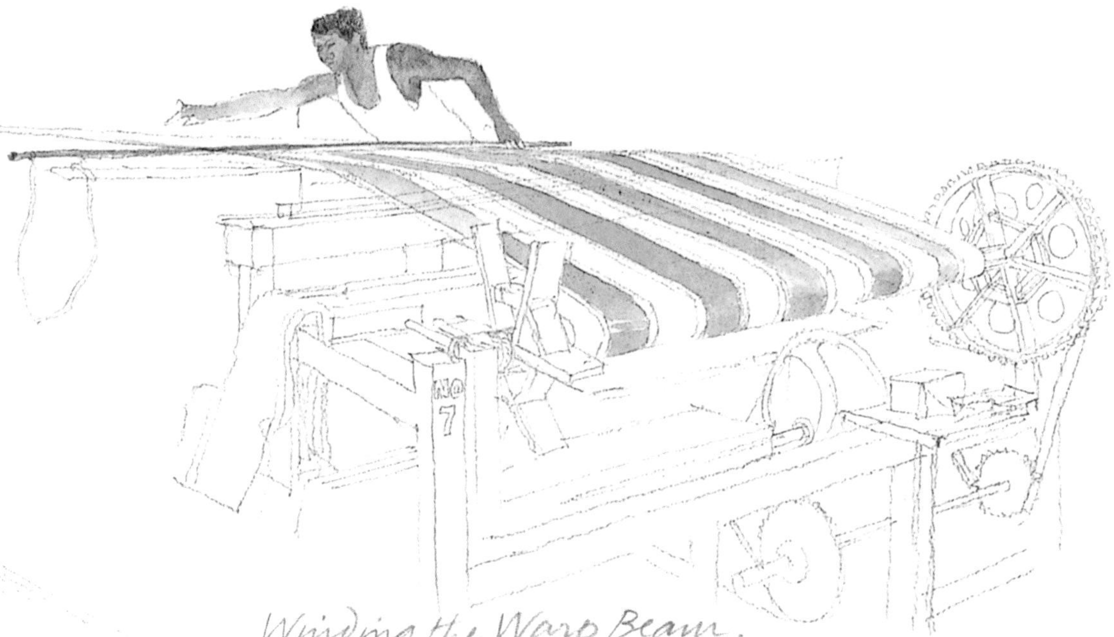

Winding the Warp Beam.

In order that the warp may be stretched on the loom, ready for the weaver, it has to be spread out and wound evenly upon a warp beam. This ensures that the individual silk yarns are cleanly separated with all kinks and knots carefully removed.

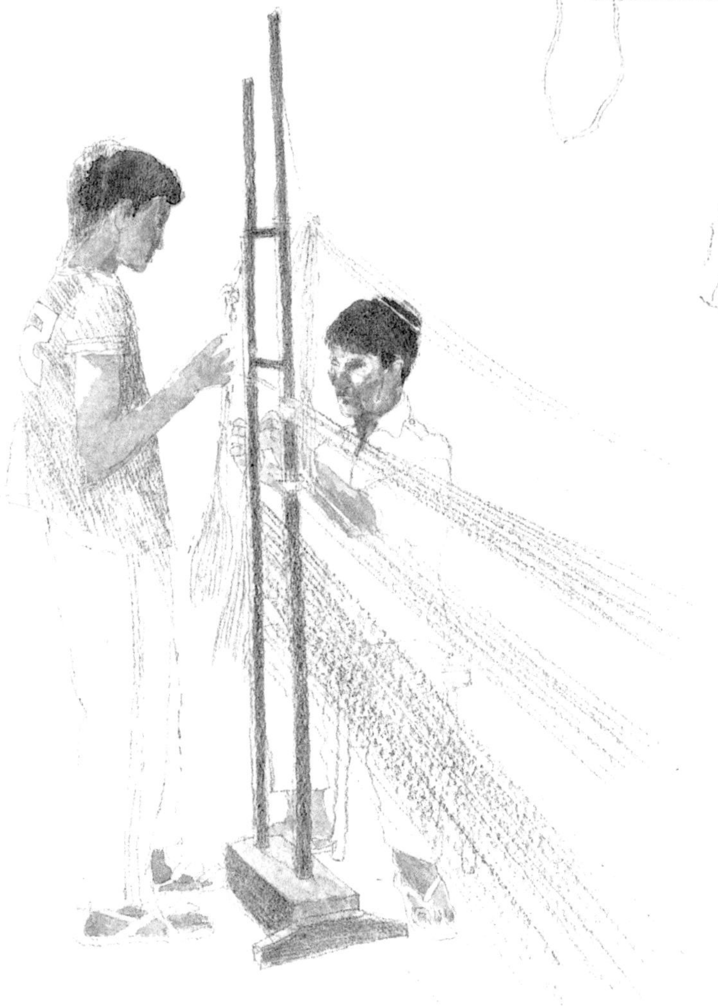

Sleying the Reed.

Sleying the reed involves the precise work of pulling each individual warp yarn between the fine teeth of a metal comb. A lightweight silk fabric can have over 2,000 warp ends, or individual silk yarns, and many hours are required to complete the task.

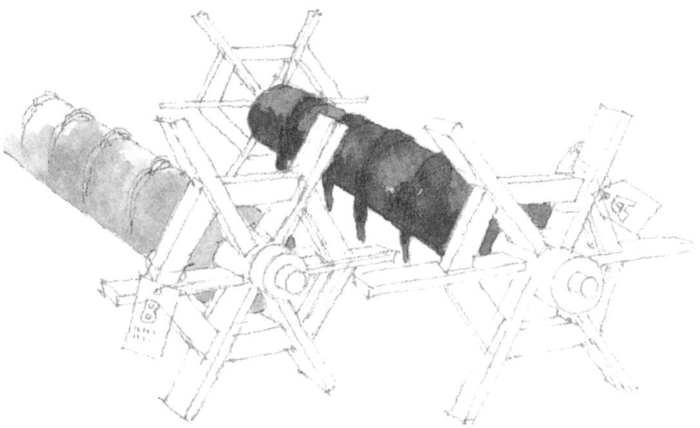

Completed warp beams are ready for storage or mounting directly on to looms for weaving.

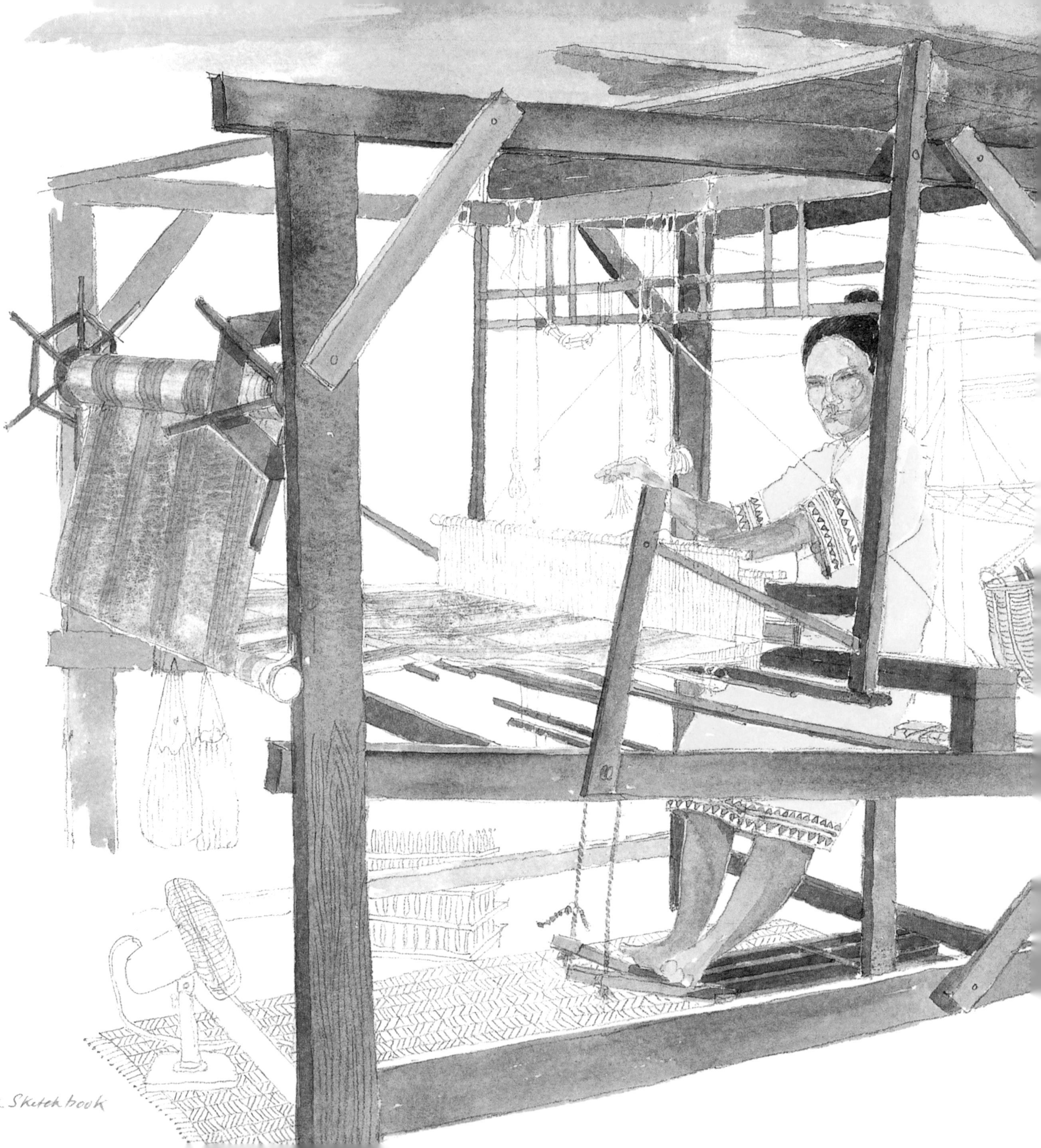

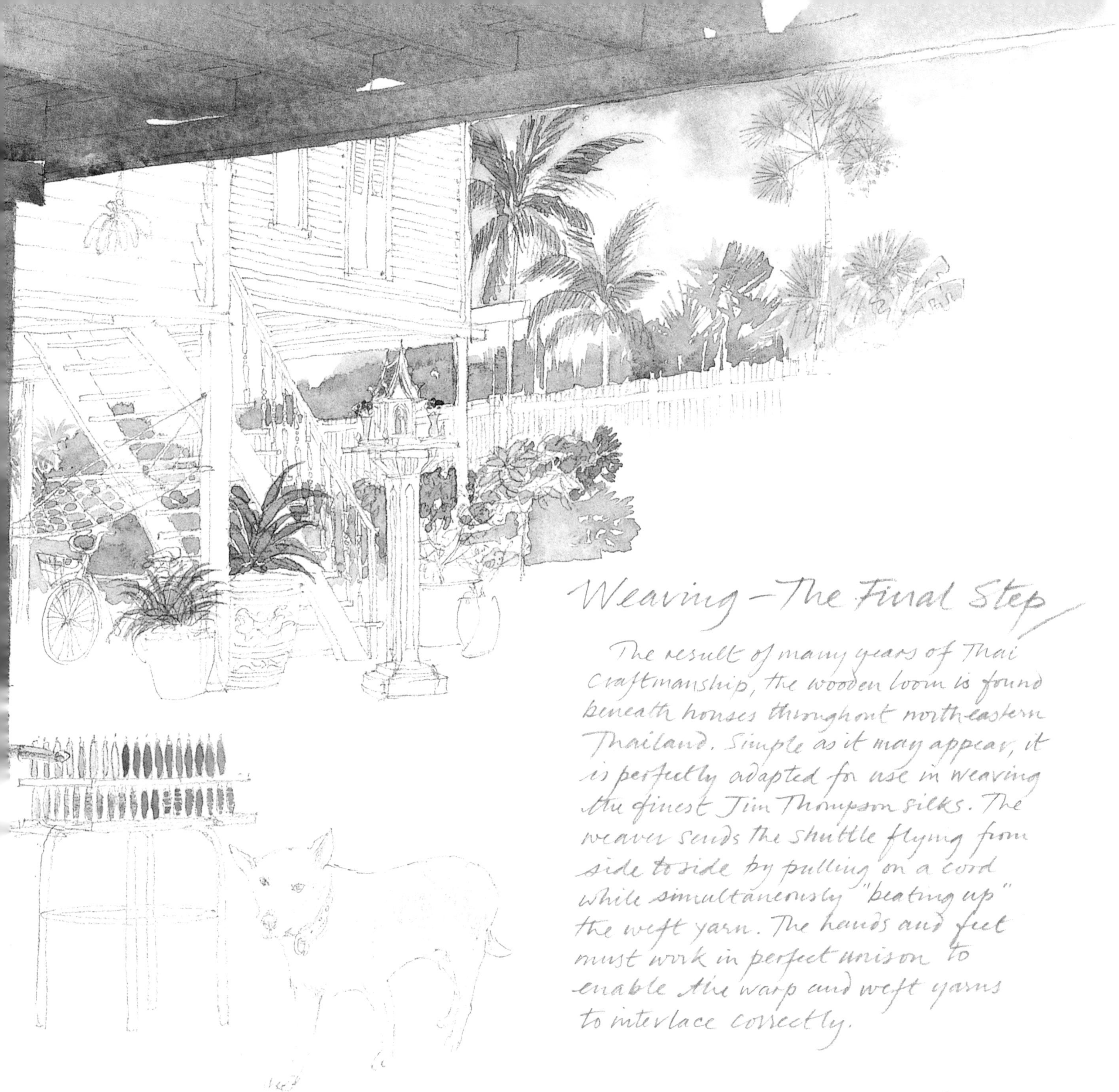

Weaving – The Final Step

The result of many years of Thai craftmanship, the wooden loom is found beneath houses throughout north-eastern Thailand. Simple as it may appear, it is perfectly adapted for use in weaving the finest Jim Thompson silks. The weaver sends the shuttle flying from side to side by pulling on a cord while simultaneously "beating up" the weft yarn. The hands and feet must work in perfect unison to enable the warp and weft yarns to interlace correctly.

The Art of Ikat

"Ikat" – a term adopted from the Malay word "mengikat," which means "to bind, tie or wrap around" – is known in Thai as "mud mii". An ancient art found in many cultures, the process involves dyeing only certain segments of the yarn, achieved by first wrapping those parts that are to remain undyed.

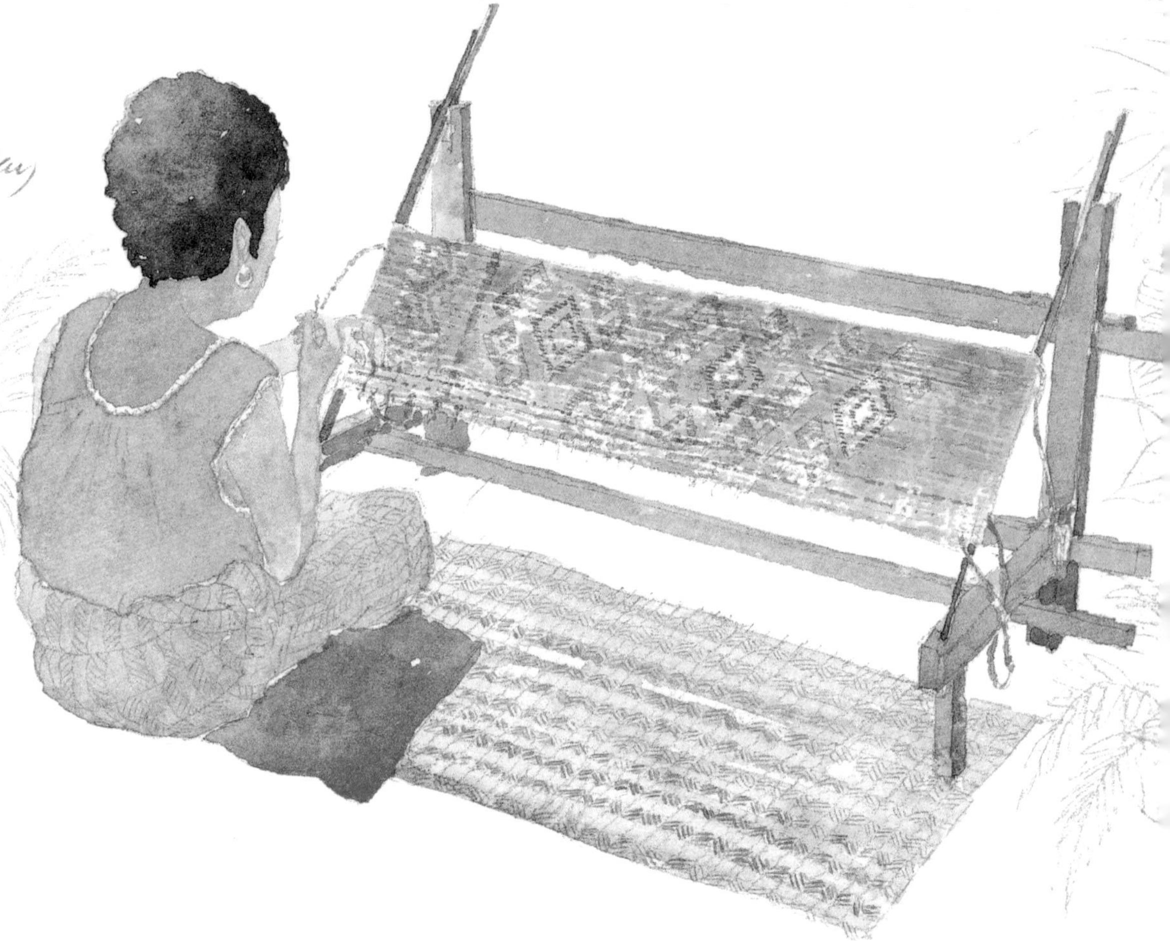

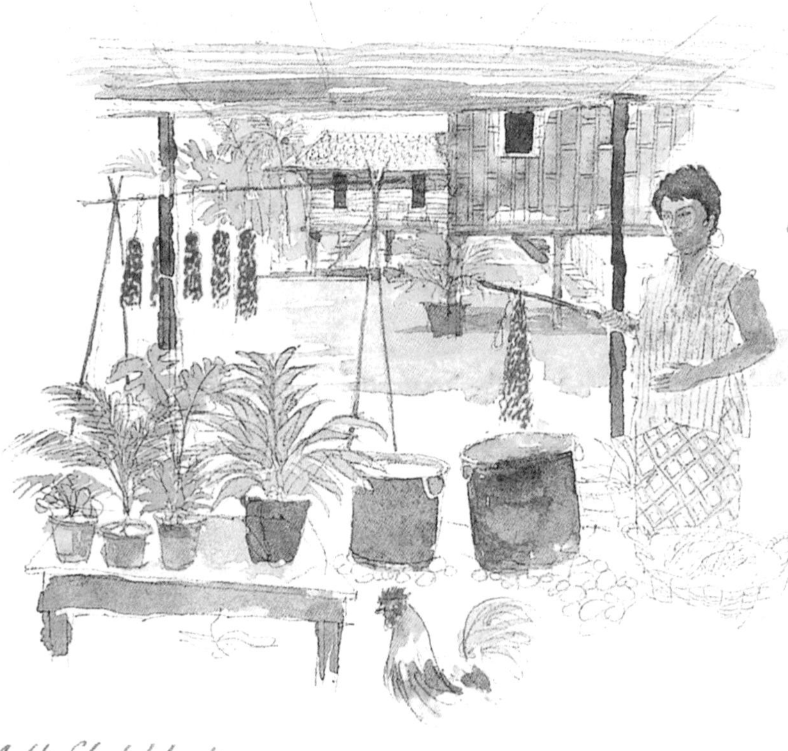

Mud mii has long been a specialty of Thailand's northeastern region. Traditionally, it was used for women's skirts and for pantaloon-like garments called "phanung," worn by both men and women. It was reserved for important occasions such as weddings and always kept stored in chests of scented wood.

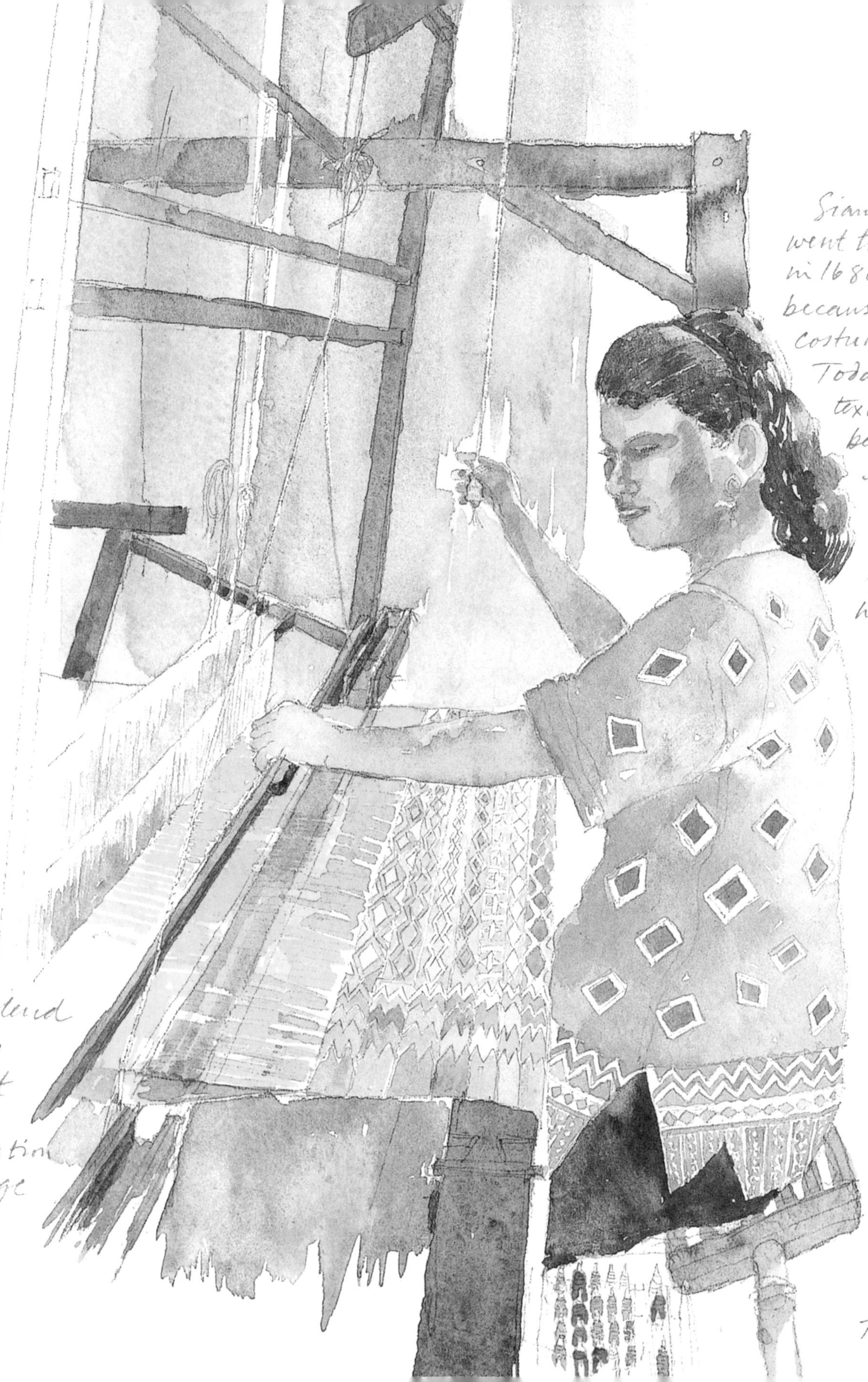

Siamese emissaries who went to the court of Louis XIV in 1686 created a sensation because of their magnificent costumes made of mudmii. Today, the elegant textiles are once more being admired for their subtle colors and wide variety of uses in fashion and in home decoration.

Weaving mudmii requires a high degree of skill and dexterity. The patterns are notable for the way the colored areas blend together in a richly textured effect that results from the differences in penetration of the dye at the edge of the wrappings.

The Craft of Weaving

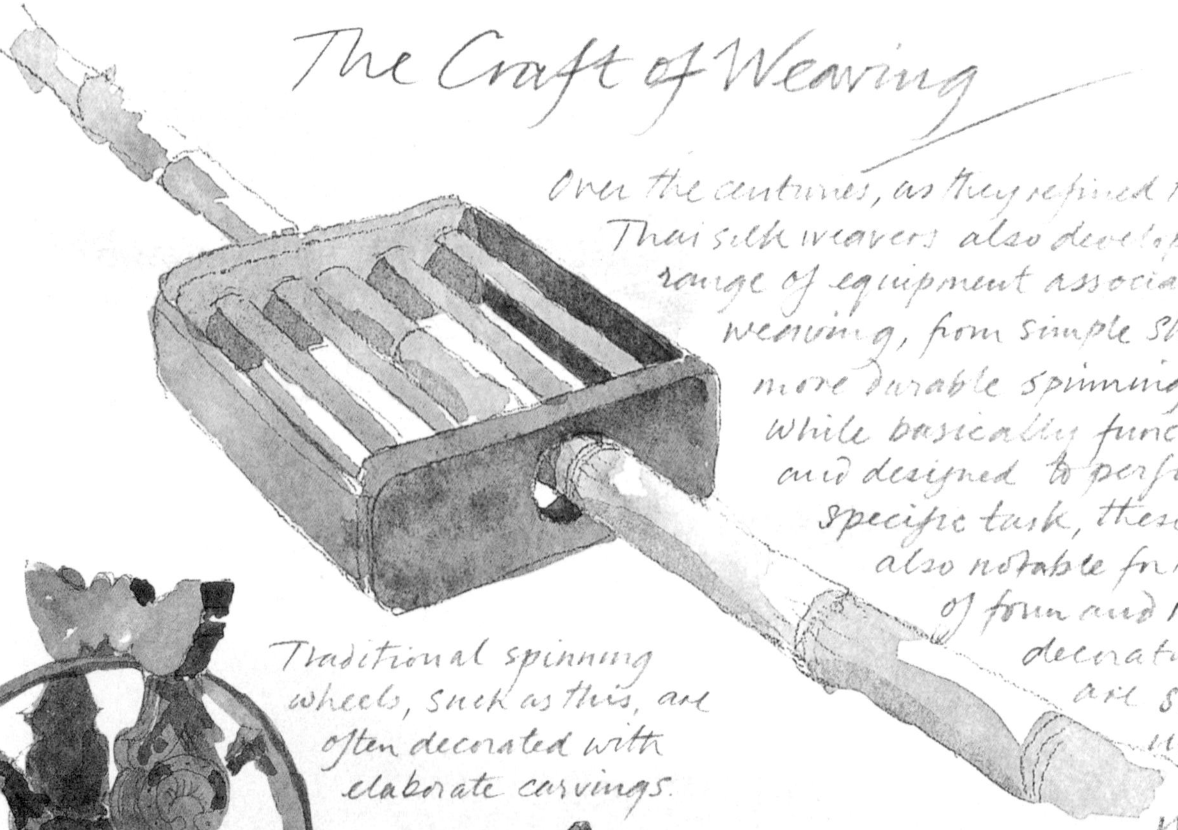

Over the centuries, as they refined their craft, Thai silk weavers also developed a wide range of equipment associated with weaving, from simple shuttles to more durable spinning wheels. While basically functional and designed to perform a specific task, these were often also notable for their elegance of form and imaginative decoration. Many are still being used in village weaving.

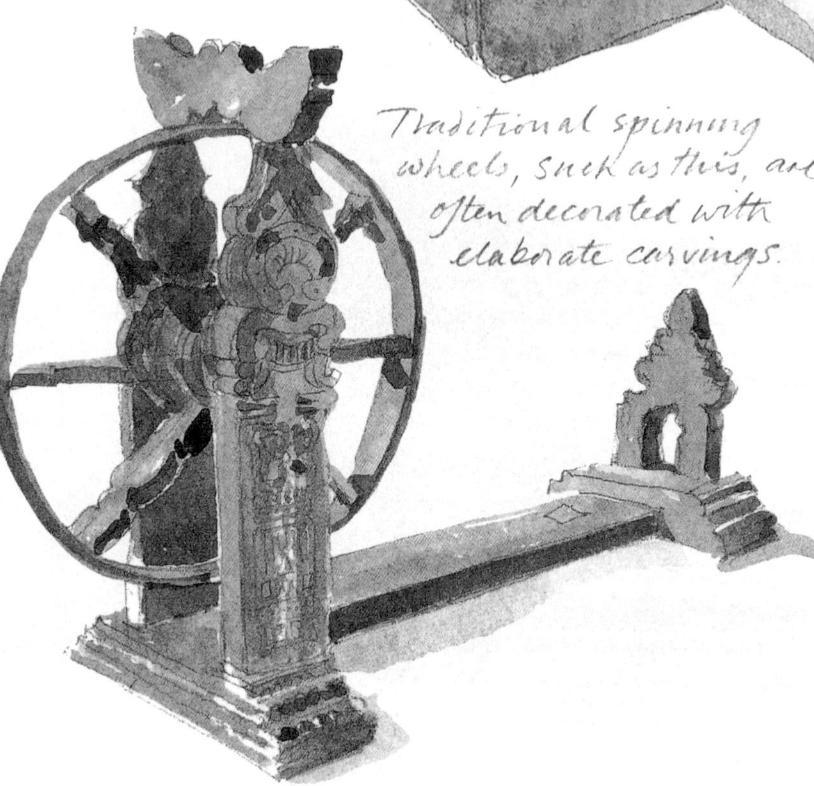

Traditional spinning wheels, such as this, are often decorated with elaborate carvings.

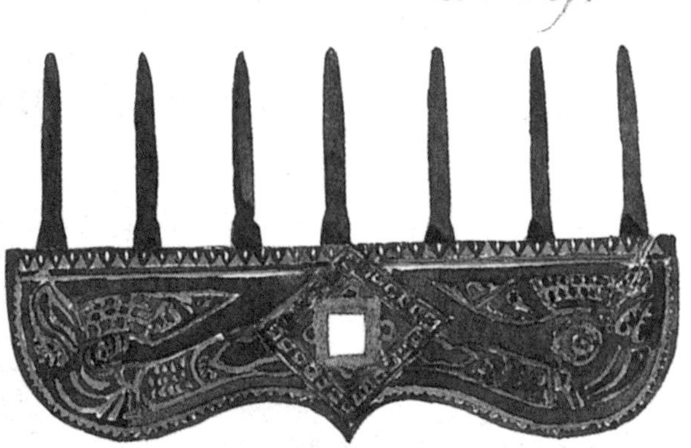

Part of a warping apparatus, used to wind warp silk.

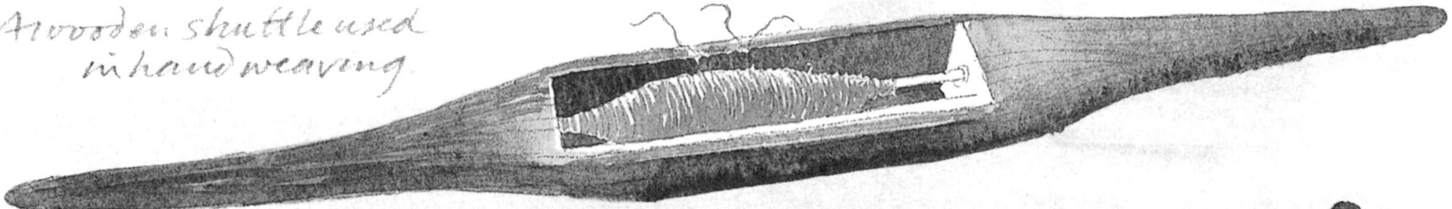
A wooden shuttle used in hand weaving

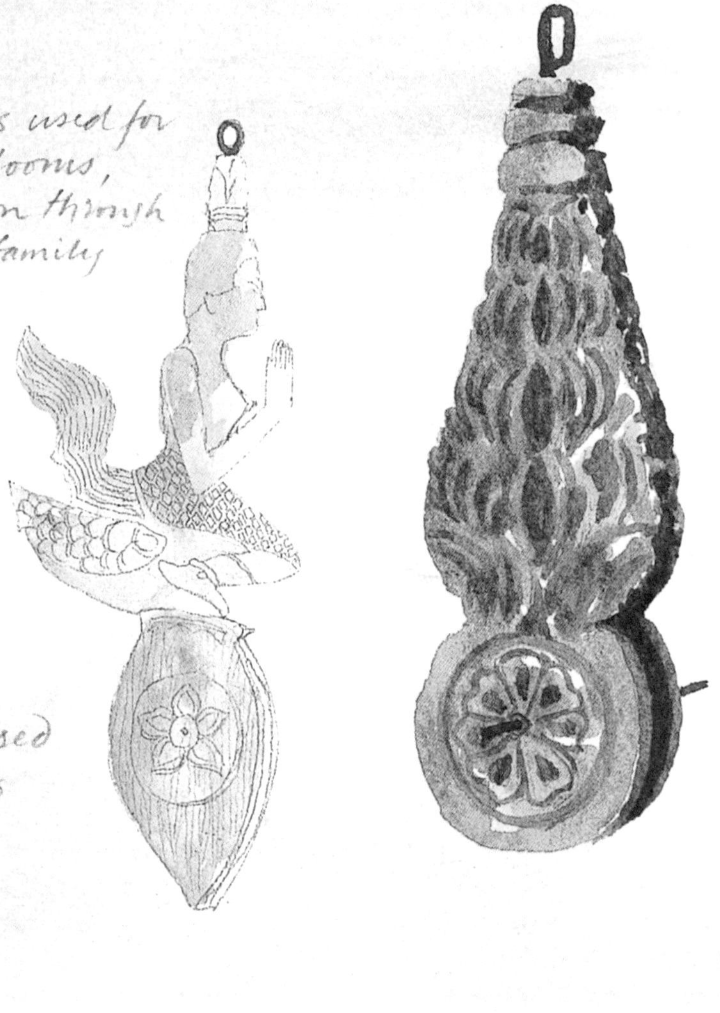
Decorative carvings used for tying harnesses on looms, often passed down through generations of family weavers.

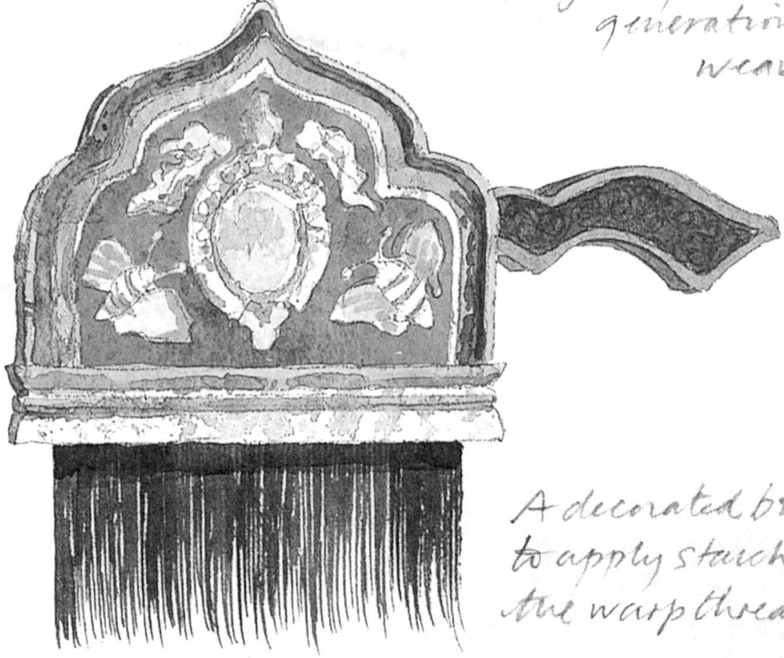
A decorated brush used to apply starch on to the warp threads

Many of the participants in the Royal Barge Procession are attired in sumptuous silk costumes.

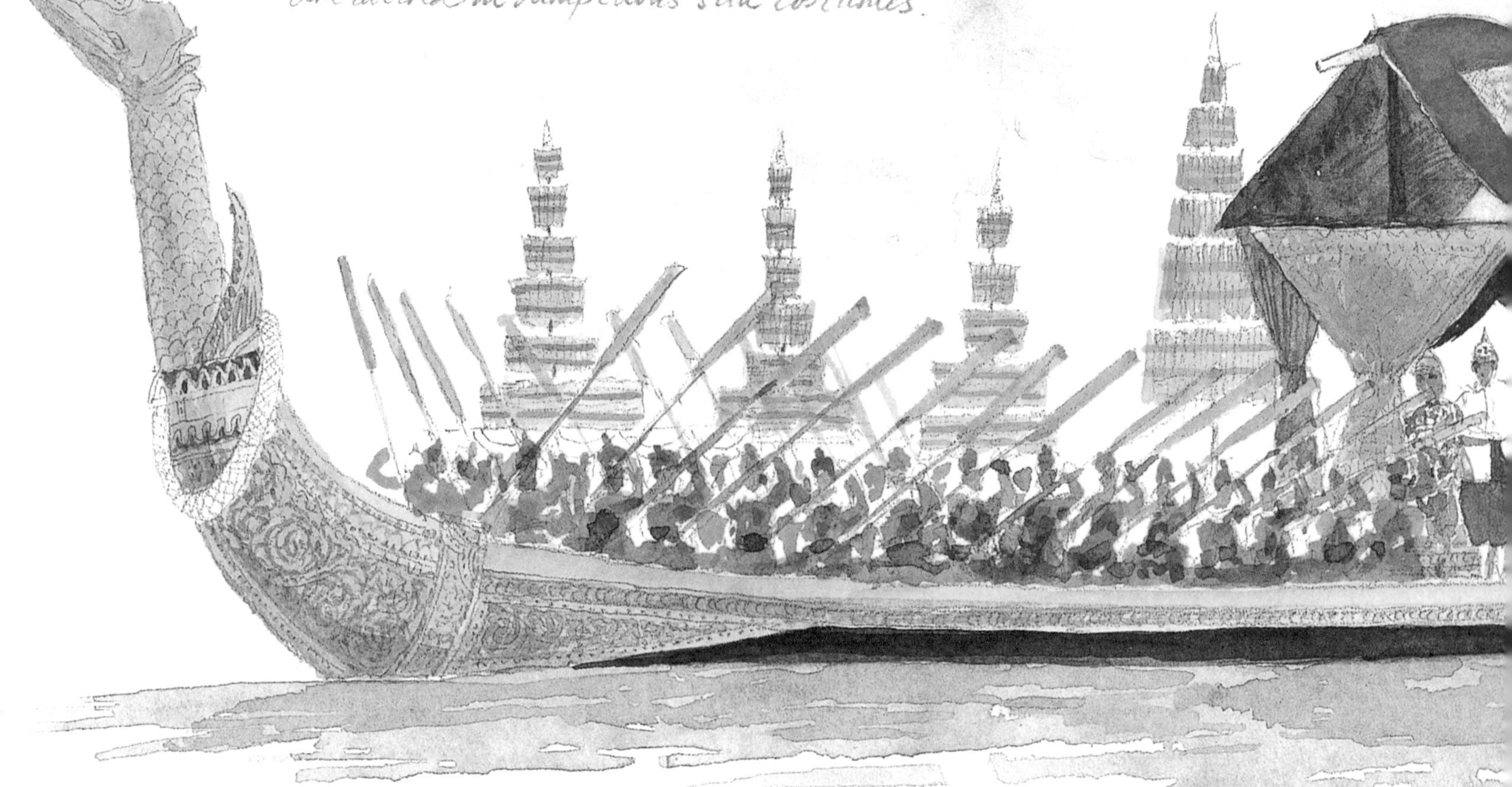

The Traditional Uses of Thai Silk

In the past, Thais wore their silks mainly for ceremonial events, whether for village functions such as weddings and temple fairs or in more rarefied circles of the royal court.

This is still true to some extent, though silk is now seen much more thanks to its greater availability and a growing awareness of its versatility.

Men wear the checkerboard patterned "pha sarong" wrapped round the lower body and tied in front. Silk pha sarongs are often woven by village girls as gifts to their future husbands for their weddings.

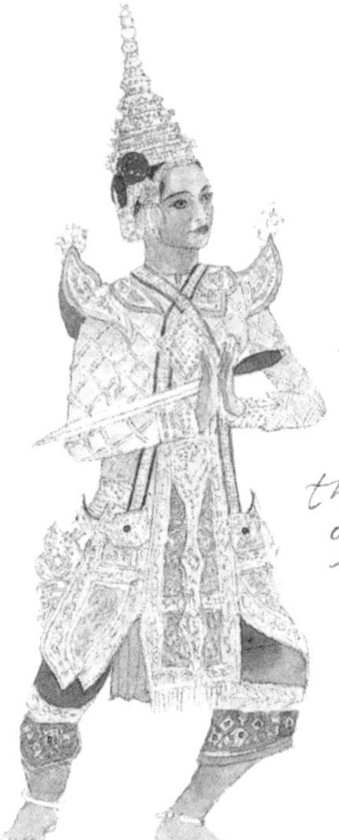

Dancers who take part in countless festivals wear traditional costumes of silk heavily encrusted with gold embroidery and glittering paste jewelry.

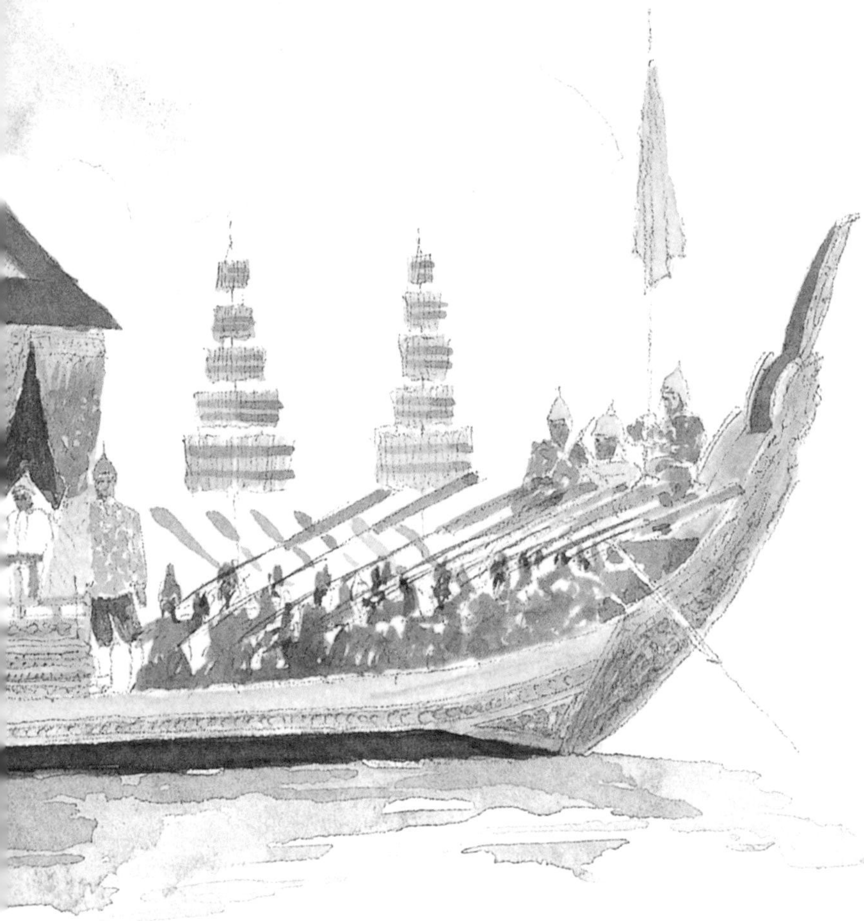

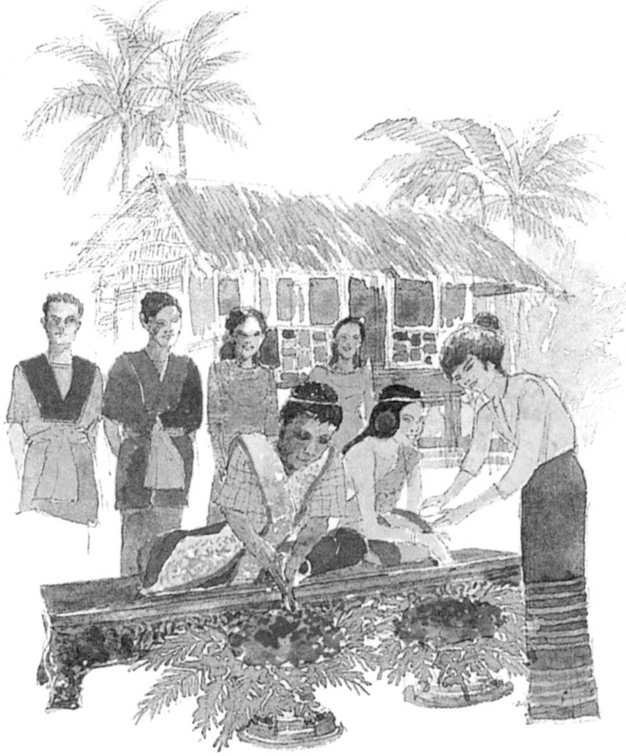

At weddings a traditional silk costume is almost a requisite for Thai brides, and many aristocratic women also wear them at important social functions. More often seen in daily life is the "pha khaw ma" nearly always cotton but in similar patterns.

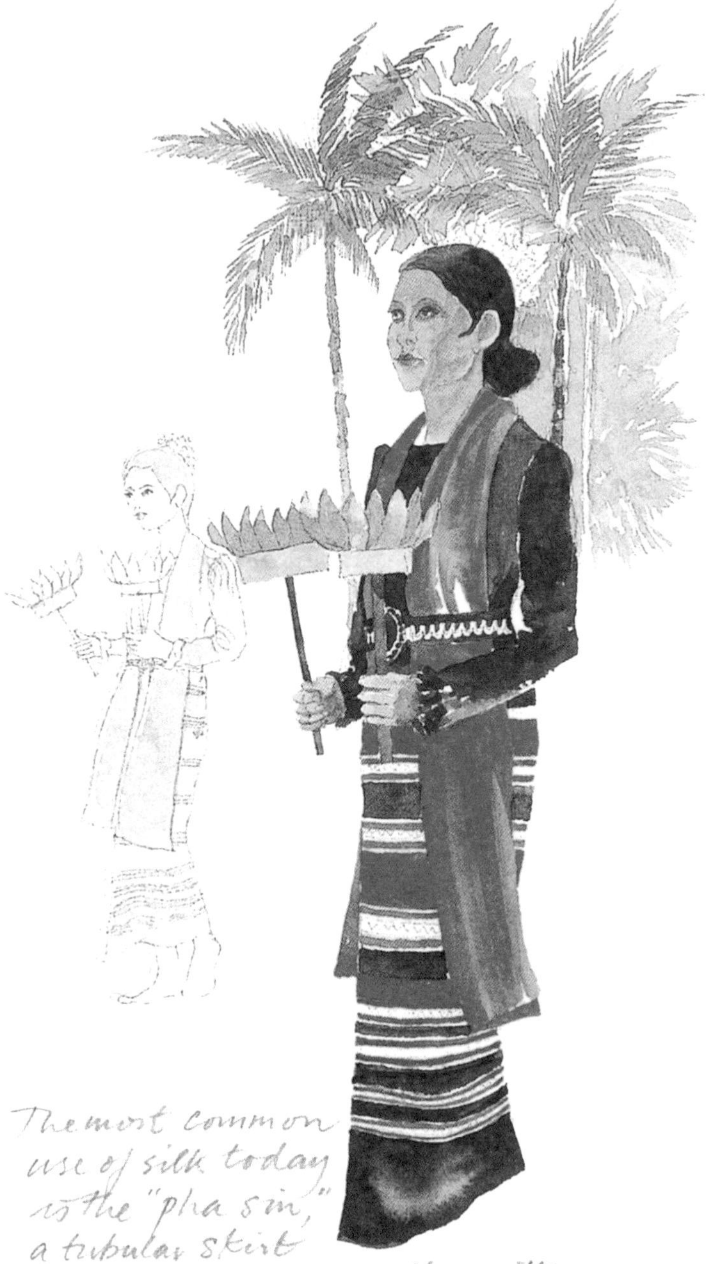

The most common use of silk today is the "pha sin," a tubular skirt worn by women together with a fitted blouse which may be plain or fancy, depending on the occasion. Usually the pha sin is divided into horizontal sections consisting of the "hua sin" (top), "tua" (body) and "tiin" (foot), which may consist of different areas on a single piece of cloth, or separate pieces sewn together.

The Bangkok Flagship

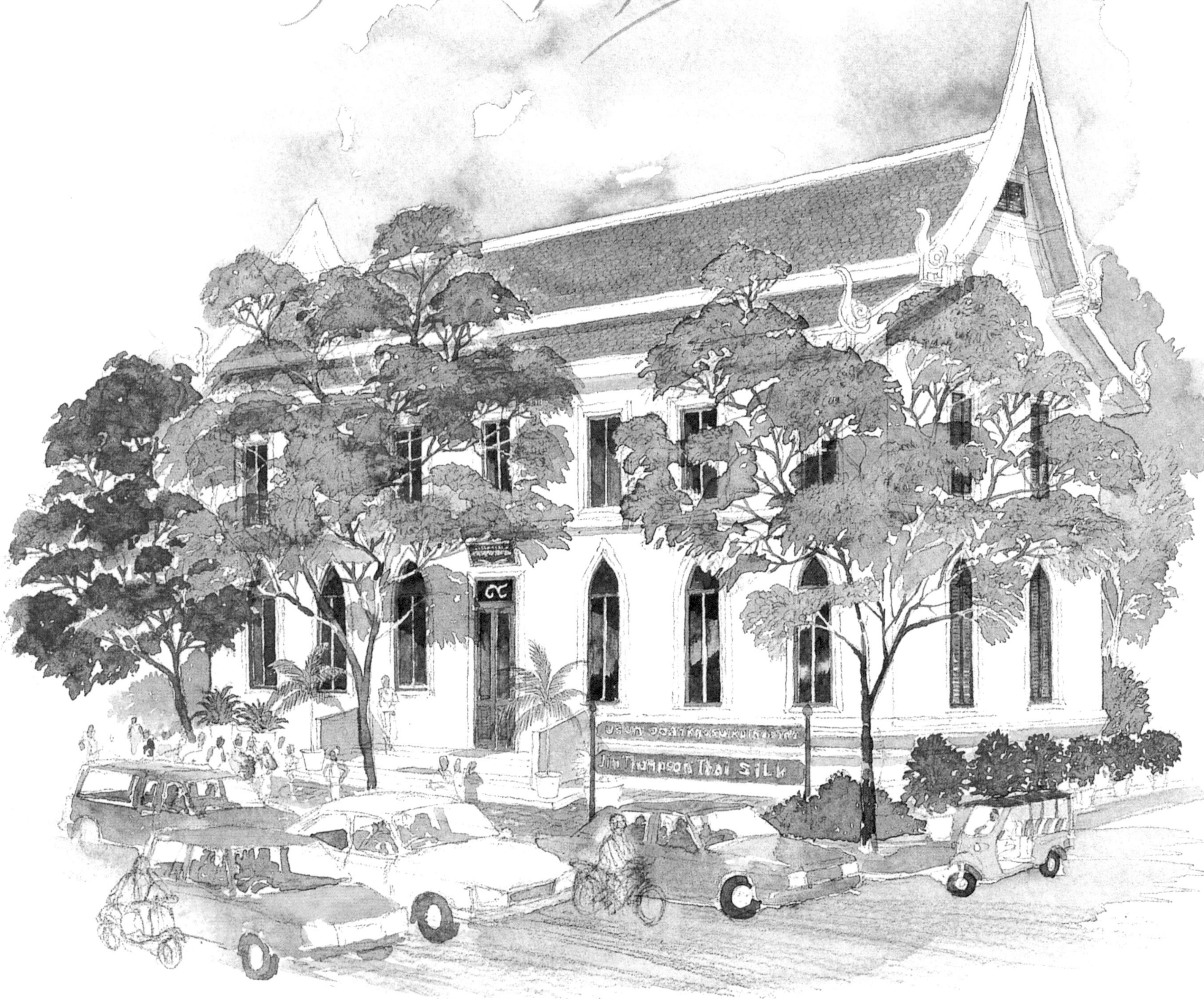

The main shop of the Jim Thompson Company, on Bangkok's Surawong Road, is an elegant building in the architectural style of 17th-century Ayutthaya. It opened in 1967, just two weeks before Jim Thompson disappeared.

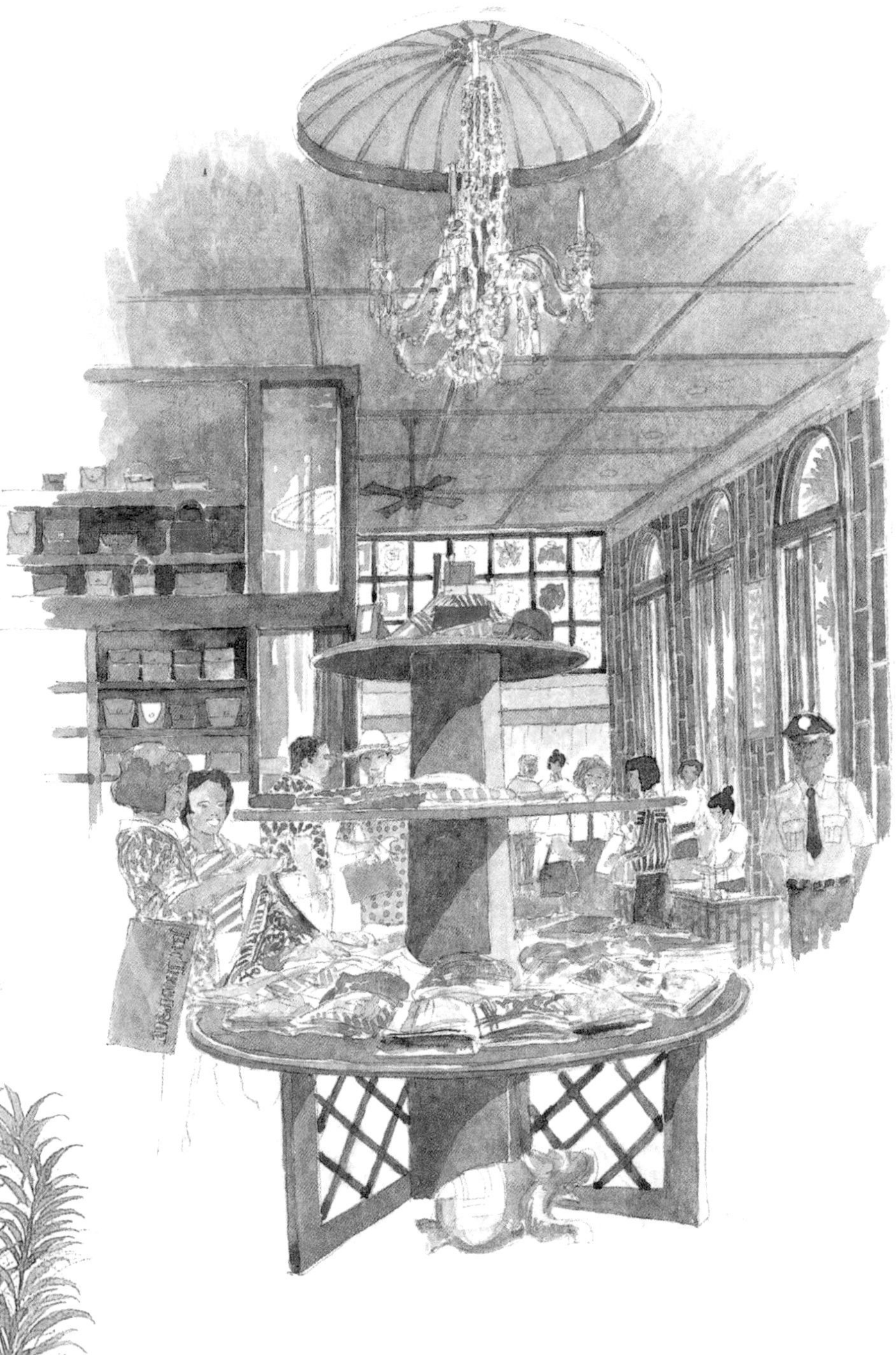

The showrooms of the shop offer a dazzling array of Thai silk in many forms, from clothing and decorative items to yardage for fashion and home furnishings.

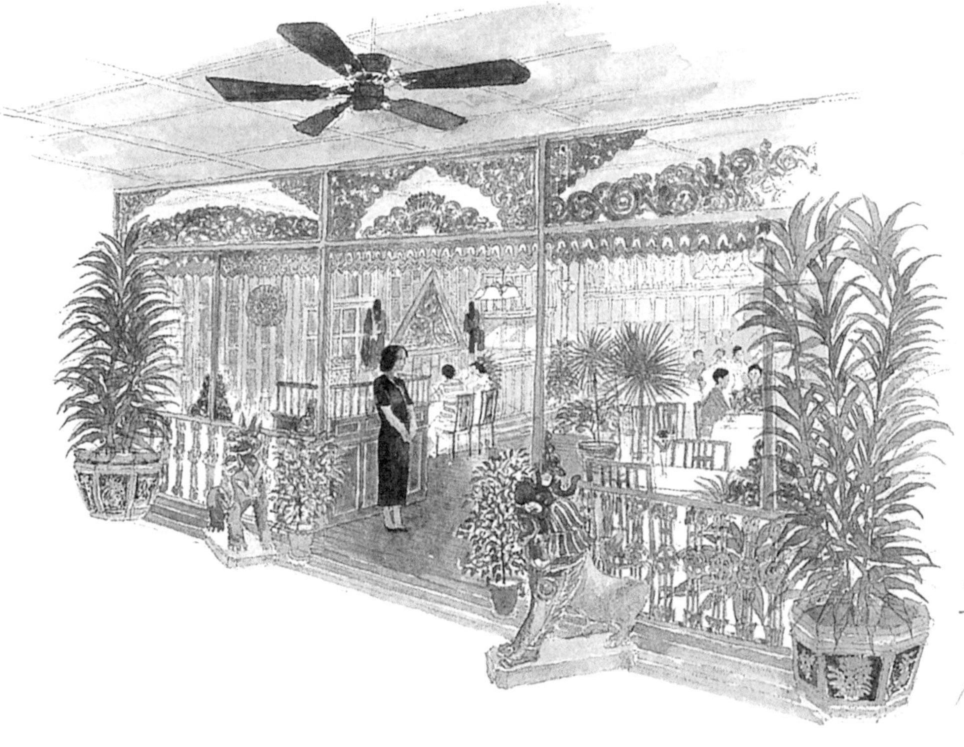

Cafe 9, a coffee shop styled after Jim Thompson's traditional Thai house, provides a pleasant place to relax on the second floor

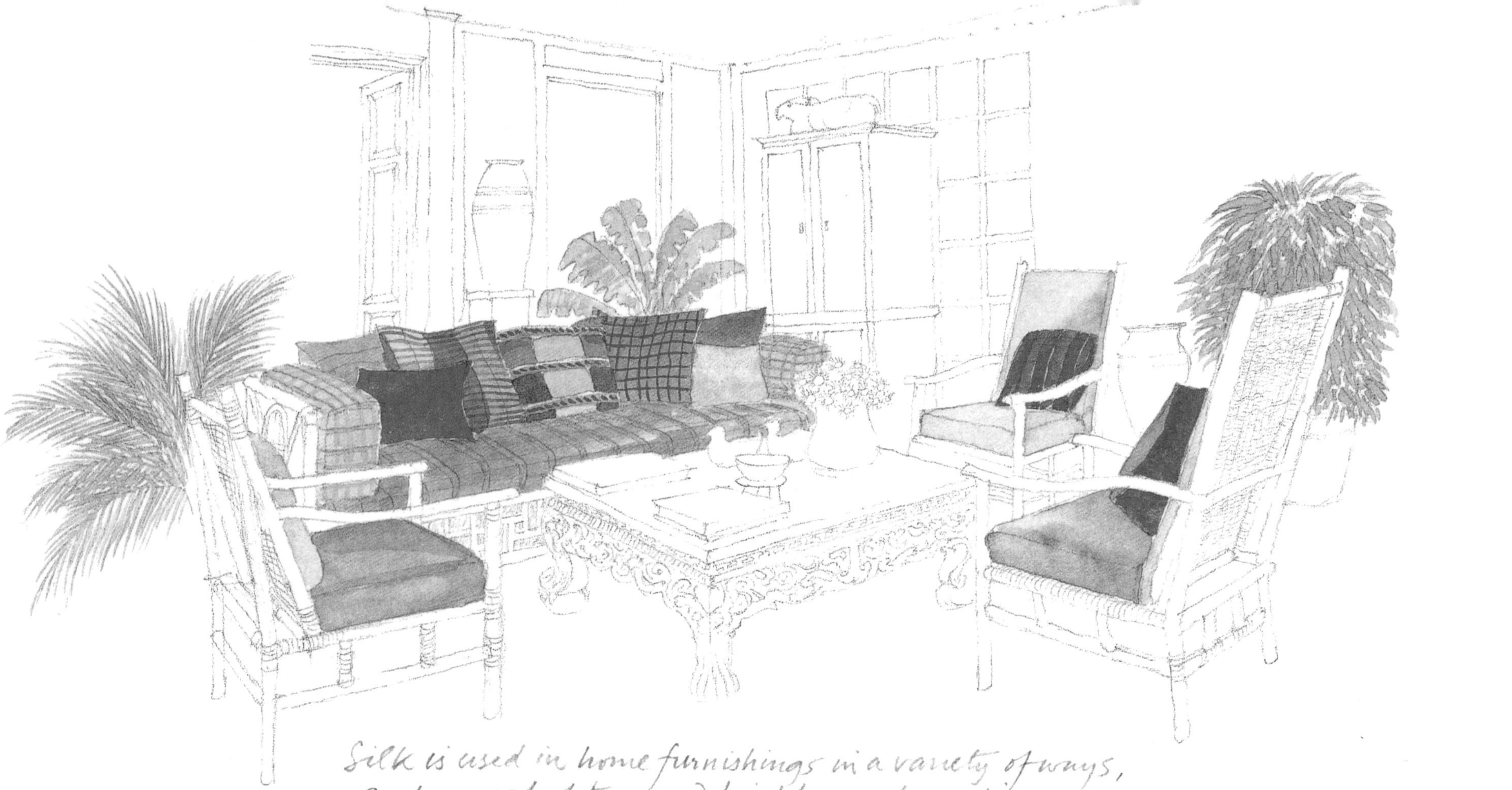

Silk is used in home furnishings in a variety of ways, such as upholstery and bright accent cushions.

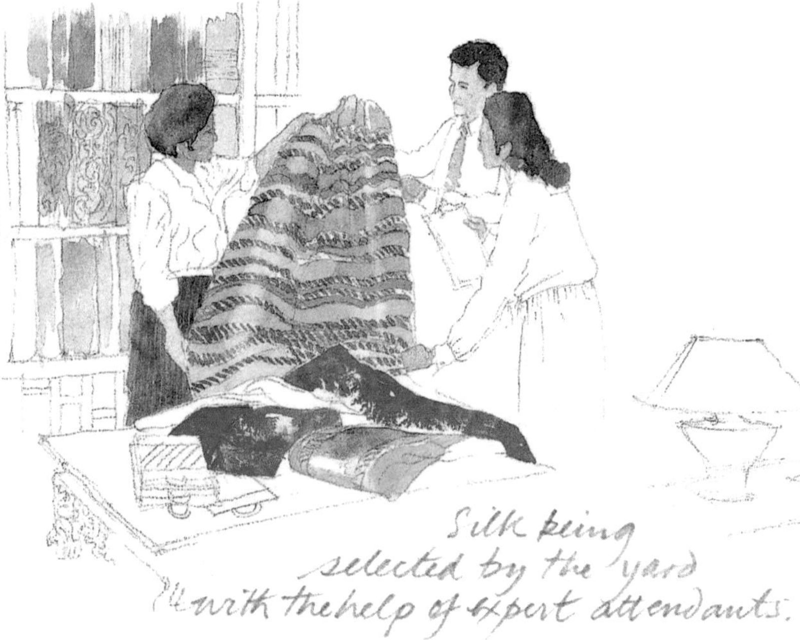

Silk being selected by the yard with the help of expert attendants.

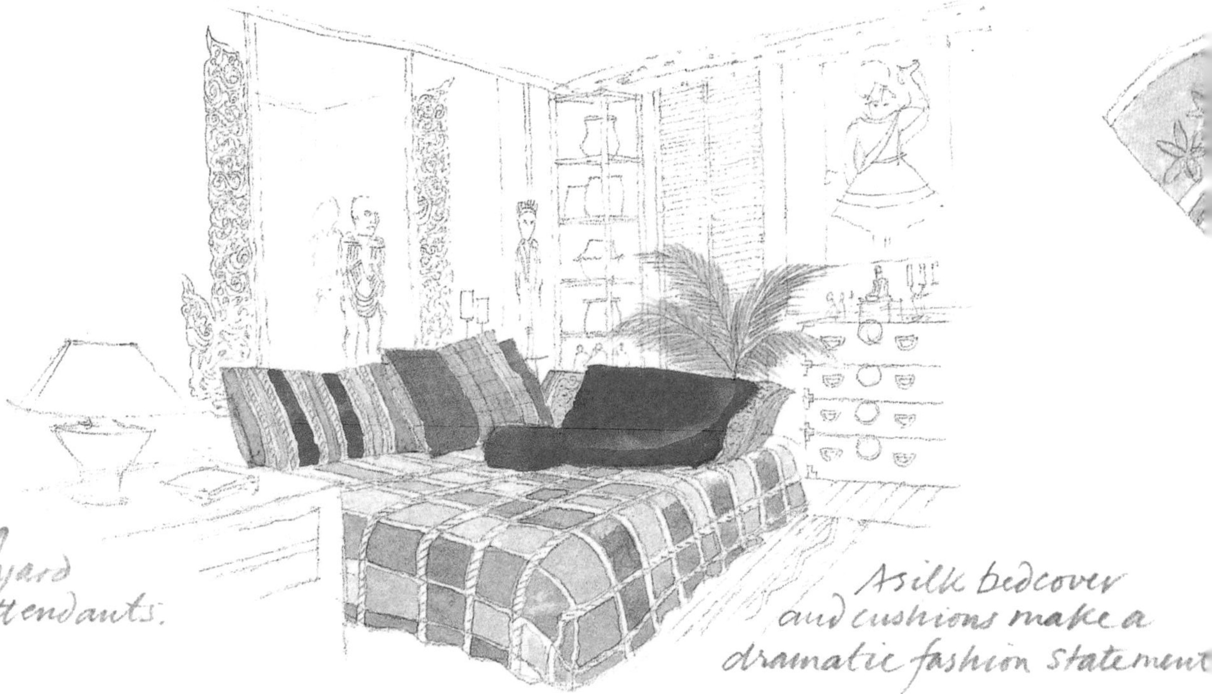

A silk bedcover and cushions make a dramatic fashion statement

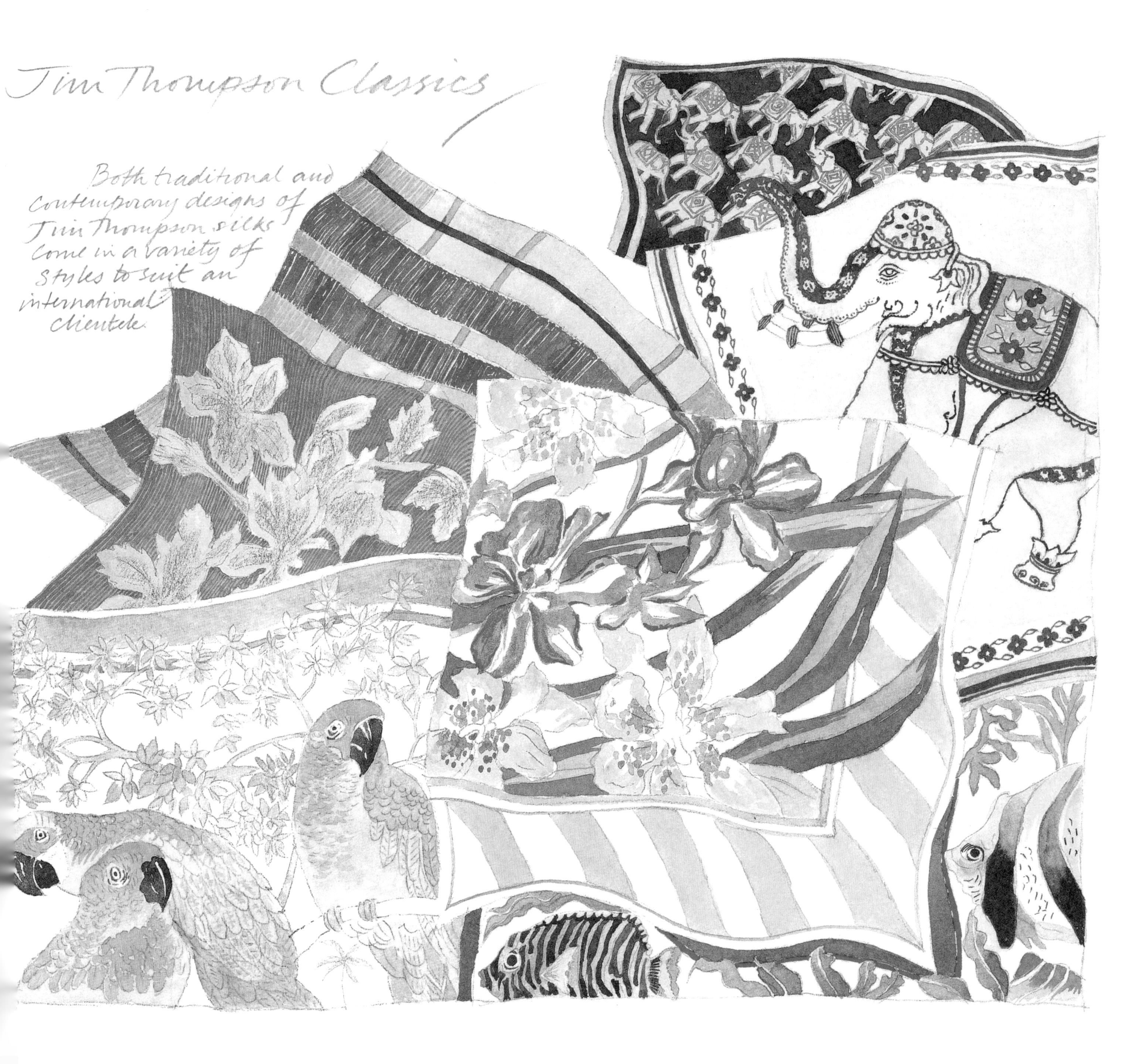
Jim Thompson Classics
Both traditional and contemporary designs of Jim Thompson silks come in a variety of styles to suit an international clientele

Jim Thompson